Fleeing Castro

DATE DUE

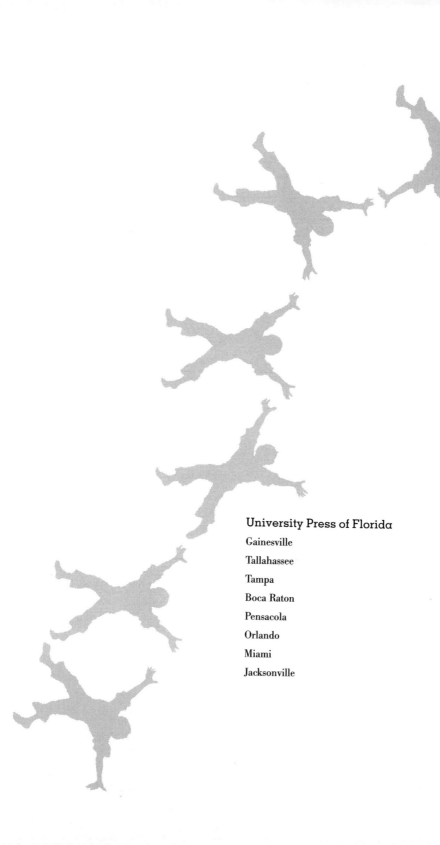

University Press of Florida

Gainesville

Tallahassee

Tampa

Boca Raton

Pensacola

Orlando

Miami

Jacksonville

Fleeing Castro

Operation

Pedro Pan

and the

Cuban

Children's

Program

Victor Andres Triay

Copyright 1998 by the Board of Regents of the State of Florida
First cloth printing, 1998
First paperback printing, 1999
Printed in the United States of America on acid-free paper
All rights reserved

03 02 01 00 99   C 6 5 4 3 2

04 03 02 01 00 99 P 6 5 4 3 2 1

Library of Congress Cataloging-in-Publication Data
Triay, Victor Andres, 1966–
Fleeing Castro: Operation Pedro Pan and the Cuban Children's
Program / Victor Andres Triay.
p. cm.
ISBN 0-8130-1612-6 (cloth)
ISBN 0-8130-1724-6 (pbk.)
1. Refugee children—Cuba. 2. Refugee children—United States.
3. Refugee children—Services for—United States. I. Title.
HV640.5.C9T74   1998   98-5942
362.87'083—dc21

The University Press of Florida is the scholarly publishing agency
for the State University System of Florida, comprising Florida
A&M University, Florida Atlantic University, Florida International
University, Florida State University, University of Central Florida,
University of Florida, University of North Florida, University of
South Florida, and University of West Florida.

University Press of Florida
15 Northwest 15th Street
Gainesville, FL 32611
http://www.upf.com

For those I have the honor of calling my family.

Contents

List of Illustrations   viii

Preface   ix

Introduction   xi

1. The Panic Begins: Cuban Parents Face a Wrenching Decision   1

2. Operation Pedro Pan: A Miami Priest Teams Up
   with a Havana Headmaster   12

3. International Intrigue: Working Out the Logistics   23

4. Behind the Iron Curtain: The Operation Inside Cuba   32

5. Helping Cubans Escape Tyranny: The Washington Details   44

6. The Cuban Children's Program: Umbrella Group Cares
   for the Wards of Pedro Pan   53

7. A Watershed Experience: Torn from Family,
   All Alone, Rescued in Miami   69

8. Toward a Resolution: Young Refugees' Reactions to Transit Centers
   and Placements   80

9. Reunited at Last: A Dream Come True
   or a Shock of Recognition?   100

10. An Evaluation: How Successful Was the Rescue Operation?   103

Appendix. Operation Pedro Pan Group, Inc.   105

Notes   107

Bibliography   117

Index   123

Illustrations

1. James Baker in his Florida home, 1994

2. Cuban children in transit center

3. Florida City girls

4. The move to the Opa-Locka barracks

5. George Guarch

6. Pedro Pan children at the airport, 1961

7. San Raphael's high school graduates, 1963

8. Sara Yaballi outside her Miami home, 1994

Illustrations follow page 60.

Preface

Fidel Castro's revolution in Cuba represents one of the more consequential events of the twentieth century. Because so many lives and institutions were affected, historians have been presented with an abundance of points of view from which to observe it. Not least among these historical perches is the Cuban Revolution's impact on U.S. immigration. From the revolution's early days—especially beginning in the summer of 1960—Cuban migration to the United States, and indeed the immigrants themselves, have played a major role in the precarious relationship between the two nations. Moreover, the exiles have thoroughly altered the social landscape of South Florida.

This book discusses the systematic migration of unaccompanied Cuban children to the United States between 1960 and 1962, dubbed by the press at the time as Operation Pedro Pan. Occurring during the first major wave of Cuban immigration, it represented the largest child refugee movement in the recorded history of the Western Hemisphere. This work also explores the Cuban Children's Program—a massive, unprecedented, nation-wide foster care system designed to provide for the children once they arrived in the United States.

To date, information pertaining to Operation Pedro Pan and the Cuban Children's Program has been scattered, inaccurate, or incomplete. It is my hope to offer a comprehensive study and interpretation of the two efforts, as well as to add a scholarly record, based on primary and secondary sources, to the existing body of knowledge in this area.

I would like to thank all those people who assisted me in the completion of this book. Because much of it appeared originally as a doctoral dissertation, it would be remiss of me not to acknowledge the substantial role of my major professor at Florida State University, Dr. William Rogers. In this world, I will never be able to repay his patience, encouragement, and guidance. An enormous debt is also owed to my parents, Andres and Maria Elena, for their constant support and example. I am likewise indebted to my wife, Emilia, for her selflessness, devotion, and understanding.

In the process of my research, the cooperation of certain people was essential. I would like to acknowledge all those who granted me interviews and assistance, especially Monsignor Bryan O. Walsh, Elisa Vilano-Chovel, Sara Yaballi, Alberto Cuartas, Gina Baena, James Baker, Margarita Fuentes, Margarita Oteiza, Juan Clark, Elena de la Torriente, Sara del Toro, Alfonso Garcia, Polita and Mongo Grau, Albertina O'Farrill, Beatrice Larin, and all those who shared with me their experiences as Pedro Pan children.

I would also like to thank the staff of the Special Collections section of the University of Miami's Otto Richter Library. On the same note, a special thanks goes out to Wesleyan University's Olin Library and its staff in Middletown, Connecticut, who so generously allow local residents to use the impressive library facilities.

Finally, I owe a debt of gratitude to the administration and staff at my place of employment, Middlesex Community College, for their help and support.

Introduction

The Caribbean island nation of Cuba entered 1959 on a wave of enthusiasm. Seven long years of an illegal dictatorship had ended with the overthrow of Fulgencio Batista and his military regime by the Twenty-Sixth of July Movement. Led by the young lawyer, politician, and former student radical Fidel Castro, the Twenty-Sixth of July Movement marched into Havana during the first few days of January and reasserted its promise of free elections and social justice for Cuba's poor. For many Cubans, it seemed a new democratic era was dawning. The thought was remote that this development would, within months, put Cuba on center stage of the cold war.

By the 1950s Cuba had achieved a relatively high standing among American nations. Consistently among Latin America's top 10 percent in standard-of-living indicators, the island boasted of its progress since the time it had achieved independence from Spain at the turn of the century—when it was among the poorest nations of the region. Cuba's economy, moreover, was much more closely tied to the U.S. economic system than to that of Latin America.

The size of Cuba's middle class was also impressive, a reflection of its economic progress. Consisting of one-third to one-fourth of the island's population, it enjoyed a level of economic security that was sorely lacking elsewhere in the region. Because of close economic ties, Cuba's middle and upper classes were likewise noted for close cultural affiliation with the United States.

Cuba's intimate ties to the United States nevertheless brought vehement opposition from a number of ideologists, whose protests of U.S. imperialism had been heard since before the turn of the century, when American investors, in the wake of the U.S. Army after the Spanish American War, significantly expanded their enterprises on the island. Although the vast majority of Cuba's wealth had been transferred from American hands to those of Cubans by the 1950s, the United States still held a great deal of influence on the island.

Cuba's notable progress during the century's first six decades, including its economic and cultural peculiarities, was offset by a sense of economic stagnation during the mid-1950s. Frustration was high among members of the middle class, who related Cuba's trouble to the limited economic potential of sugar, the island's main source of wealth. Moreover, the island's countryside was home to thousands of destitute peasants for whom Cuba's economic progress meant little. Hundreds of thousands of other poor people lived in abject poverty in shantytowns outside Havana and other cities. There was also political frustration in Cuba. The corrupt democratic regimes of the 1940s had opened the door to an equally corrupt dictatorship in the 1950s. In all these areas, the Cuban public—rich and poor alike—sought a remedy. Castro's revolution seemed to promise just that.

Castro's various early governments in 1959 included members of his movement as well as important bourgeois liberal politicians. The revolutionary government's first major act, in lieu of holding its promised elections, was to rid the island of Batista's administration. In hindsight, it is clear that the trials during the spring and summer of 1959 gave some indication of the totalitarianism to come. Jacobin-style trials were held under the public eye, often in large stadiums, broadcast to the entire island. Batista officials were dragged before military courts and summarily convicted amid cries of "Paredon!" (To the execution wall!) from frenzied crowds waving Cuban flags and other banners. Photographs of the mutilated bodies of those executed were circulated throughout the island, with the dual purpose of satisfying the public's bloodlust and sending a veiled message to those who opposed—or who might oppose—the Castro government. That form of intimidation set a precedent for a regime that would use terror as its chief weapon in securing overt support from the public.

By the autumn of 1959, many Cubans had become wary of Castro. His inclusion of Communist party members in his governments and the purging of liberals seemed to indicate to many that the revolution was taking a drastic turn to the left. Accusations of Communist infiltration from both opponents and former supporters were substantiated when Hubert Matos, Camaguey Province's military governor and a former Castro guerrilla, was sentenced to prison for his respectful criticism of Castro's inclusion of Communists.

Castro's actions over the next year further confirmed the fears of Matos and others. Having abandoned traditional reformist ideology and ballot-box democracy, the regime began enacting certain policies that would directly set the revolution on its new course—the establishment of a totali-tarian, Communist state personified by Fidel Castro. The achievement of that goal required both the destruction of nonrevolutionary institutions and the elimination of all opposition.

Among Castro's first moves was to put his relations with the Soviet Union and other Eastern bloc nations on a more intimate level. Knowing that the United States (which had initially supported the revolution) would oppose his turn toward Marxism, he used the Soviet shield to forestall any American attempts to overthrow his government. In time, the Soviets would become close allies and sustain the Castro regime both eco-nomically and militarily. In 1960 Castro also began nationalizing foreign and Cuban-owned businesses on the island. Moreover, backed by the new-found friendship with the USSR, his revolutionary rhetoric became in-creasingly hostile toward the United States and those that the regime broadly defined as the native bourgeoisie. During this period, freedom of the press, freedom of assembly, the right to a writ of habeas corpus, and the University of Havana's autonomy were destroyed. Likewise, the Castro regime intervened in and either shut down or revolutionized the labor unions, professional associations, private clubs, and, in 1961, Cuba's pub-lic and private school system.

Castro's assault on the Old Regime was carried out by Cubans involved in revolutionary organizations such as the Committees for the Defense of the Revolution (an organization of neighborhood watchdog groups that aimed to root out opposition) and by an armed citizen's militia, the regular army, the G.2 (political police), and bureaucratic puppets. With the revo-lutionary regime's backing, these groups subdued opponents. Their activi-ties ranged from home searches of suspected counterrevolutionaries and interventions in private organizations, to taunting religious worshippers.

The strength of Castro's personality and the near-mystic veneration of him by a significant percentage of the public secured enough support for the leader to carry out his aims.

By late 1960 the battle lines in Cuba had been drawn. Those who opposed Communism were victimized and oppressed by the regime and were left with few choices. Many fled into exile. Some joined underground counterrevolutionary groups. Without a military base of their own, and given that it was Communism they were battling, many looked to the United States for help. For its part, the U.S. government—angered by the confiscation of American property and threatened by the geopolitical consequences of Castro's newfound friendship with the USSR—began taking an increasingly hard line against the Cuban regime. While arming Cuban counterrevolutionaries and supporting exile-led flights over Cuba, President Eisenhower lowered Cuba's sugar quota in 1960 so as to pressure Castro. That action only led to the latter's tighter embrace of the USSR and hastened his commitment to Communism. Diplomatic relations were finally broken in January 1961.

Events in Cuba had profound consequences for the United States. In the first place, cold war attention had now been shifted to the Western Hemisphere—only ninety miles from American soil. Second, and of lasting consequence, events ignited a mass migration out of Cuba. The United States provided sanctuary for the overwhelming majority of exiles from Castro's Cuba, thereby becoming further entangled.

Among those fleeing Cuba during the early 1960s were more than 14,000 unaccompanied children. Their exodus, mirroring that of other Cuban exiles, was a response to the totalitarian Communist state being imposed by Castro. Parents, fearing that the revolution would devour their children, entrusted their fate to government and religious agencies in the United States. Not only did these children represent the largest child refugee movement in the recorded history of the Western Hemisphere, but also the program designed to care for them, the Cuban Children's Program, revolutionized many aspects of social service provision in the United States. Furthermore, the U.S. government and the Catholic Church in the United States—in what the press dubbed Operation Pedro Pan—assisted the anti-Castro underground in the semisecret effort to smuggle the children from the island, an operation that made events all the more intriguing.

One

The Panic Begins:
Cuban Parents Face
a Wrenching Decision

Fidel Castro wanted to be the father of my children.
Samuel Teurbe Tolon

Fidel Castro's embrace of Marxism-Leninism came as a considerable shock to many Cubans. Although Castro did not officially announce his turn toward Communism for several months, he began reshaping Cuba along such lines during the summer and fall of 1960. Until that time, most Cubans seeking exile in the United States had been either Batista supporters or politically active in some other way. Others represented the island's largest landowners, who were affected by the revolution's early agrarian reform laws.

During the reforms accompanying Cuba's conversion into a Communist state in mid-1960, the composition of the exiles, as well as their condition, changed significantly. No longer limited to former Batista officials, the refugees represented a broader segment of the population and were fleeing not because of Batista's ouster but because of Castro's imposition of a Marxist system. With some considerable exceptions, they were middle-, upper-middle-, and upper-class Cubans. Nearly all of them were destitute, as the Castro regime began restricting the amount of money and possessions that could be taken away from the island. This first large wave of Cuban migration lasted until the Cuban missile crisis of October 1962, when commercial airline flights between the United States and Cuba were canceled.

It was during that first wave of Cuban migration to the United States that Operation Pedro Pan occurred. The exodus of unaccompanied children officially commenced in December 1960, as the result of a meeting between Father Bryan Walsh, the head of Miami's Catholic Welfare Bureau, and James Baker, the headmaster of an American school in Cuba with connections to the anti-Castro underground. They focused on helping the Cuban underground secure proper exit papers and, if necessary, airline tickets for Cuban children whose parents sought to send them into U.S. exile. At about the same time, Walsh developed the rudiments of the Cuban Children's Program, designed to care for those children who lacked relatives or friends with whom they could stay once they arrived in the United States. The role of Father Walsh and James Baker will be studied in greater detail in subsequent chapters.

Although all socioeconomic groups were represented among the unaccompanied children, the majority were from middle-class backgrounds. The wealthy, having been affected earlier in the revolution, for the most part had obtained the proper documentation to leave Cuba before the strained diplomatic relations between Havana and Washington made such a simple request nearly impossible to fulfill. The low number of poor children in Operation Pedro Pan was no doubt due to a lack of financial resources. Moreover, because of Castro's promises to help their class, Cuba's poor were by and large enthusiastic about the changes taking place on the island. After years of social and economic exclusion, their sudden enfranchisement made many hopeful for a brighter future under the new regime. A number of Cuba's poor would find themselves fleeing in future migratory waves.

The reasons why so many middle-class parents sent their children into exile were varied and compelling. Generally speaking, the specter of Communism was terrifying for many Cubans, especially those of the middle and upper classes. Not only did they stand to lose economically, socially, and politically under Communism but for generations they had learned to fear it. One source of their preexisting fear was their close economic and cultural ties with the United States, which had itself been engaged for over a decade in leading the global struggle against Communism, both militarily and by means of propaganda.

The influence of religious institutions was likewise important. Although the Catholic Church in Cuba never penetrated the hearts and souls of the masses as it did in other Latin American nations, it indeed held considerable influence among the middle and upper classes, especially through the Catholic schools that many such people attended. Because Cuba's clergy were largely Spaniards and Americans, generations of Catholic schoolchildren and others closely connected to the church before 1959 received fervently anti-Communist instruction. For their part, the Americans supplied a large number of nuns, whose orders ran numerous girls' schools on the island. A group of American priests from Philadelphia's Villanova University operated a university by the same name in Havana. The anti-Communist ideologies of both the U.S. government and the Holy See quite naturally filtered through to Cubans with whom the representatives of the church came in contact. The Spanish Catholic Church, which supplied the majority of Cuba's priests and nuns, had felt the sting of anticlericalism during the Spanish Civil War (1936–39) a generation earlier and was thus probably even more committed to spreading the gospel of anti-Communism.

Cuba also had a number of Protestant schools and churches, many of them founded by American missionaries earlier in the century. Even though most were administered by Cubans by 1959, the dependence of many on American denominations exposed them to anti-Communist values, as was evident also in secular schools run by Americans in Cuba.

Despite the images of Communist bogeymen being burned into the collective consciousness of upper- and middle-class Cubans, it would be erroneous to assume that those who made the monumental decision to leave the island in exile did so for that reason alone. In truth, the nature of the revolution was such that it directly affected the lives of those Cubans in negative ways. Fagen, Brody, and O'Leary state in their work, *Cubans in Exile: Disaffection and the Revolution,* that self-imposed exile arises from the confluence of four phenomena: (1) the perception of life's conditions as being intolerable or about to become so, (2) the attribution of this state of things to the incumbent regime, (3) the ability to conceive of an alternate place of residence and a means to get there, and (4) the existence of such an alternative.[1] Families who took advantage of Operation Pedro Pan—and in fact all exiles of the period—met those criteria.

The first unaccompanied children sent to the United States via Operation Pedro Pan were those of anti-Castro underground operatives. A large number of counterrevolutionaries had been active Castro supporters before the leader's shift toward Communism. Believing that he had sold out the revolution, they took up arms against him. Others who fought Castro had been politically inactive before the revolution. Nevertheless, they were all determined to prevent a Communist takeover of Cuba.

The men and women who joined the effort to overthrow Castro took risks that included endangering their lives. Because the G.2 had infiltrated the highest levels of the underground, anti-Castro activities became extremely hazardous. In a common occurrence during those years, armed guards might appear at a home at any time and detain a member of the household. Although members of the underground were willing to accept those risks, they understandably feared the consequences for their children if they were caught. As many Cubans had close ties to Spain, one point of reference was the Spanish Civil War. From that conflict emerged stories of Republican forces sequestering children of opposition leaders until those leaders surrendered themselves—a horrifying prospect for any thoughtful parent. Hence, a large number of underground operatives agreed to fight Castro only if their children were out of the regime's reach.

Another parental fear about active opposition to Castro concerned teenagers involved in anti-Castro activities. Counterrevolutionary youths were prevalent in organizations such as Juventud Estudiantil Catolica (Catholic Students' Youth) and the Juventud Obrera Catolica (Catholic Workers' Youth). Many Catholic secondary school students were also active in resistance to the regime.[2] Counterrevolutionary activities among youths might have ranged from symbolic gestures, such as marches or overt defiance of revolutionary principles, to participation in armed resistance. Fearing that their children might thus endanger themselves and the lives of their families, many parents viewed sending them away from Cuba as not only a viable but highly desirable solution.

Another parental fear was the perceived certainty of civil war. Again considering the precedent of the Spanish Civil War, many parents sought to protect their children by preemptively moving them out of the war zone. Even more important, parents feared the state would draft their teenage sons into the military. Not only would that put the youngsters in danger, but for parents opposed to the regime, it would mean their sons being forced to fight for the side of their adversaries. Moreover, being drafted into the military by the state could have resulted in Communist indoctrination of teenagers. Since the draft age in Cuba was fifteen, many parents sent their sons away before they reached that age. In fact, a disproportionate amount of the children sent out of Cuba in Operation Pedro Pan were teenage boys.[3] A connection with the military draft must be assumed. Such drastic measures to protect teenage boys by sending them into exile lasted well into the late 1960s.

Parents who took advantage of Operation Pedro Pan were motivated by reasons other than physical safety, however. The Castro revolution's pervasiveness was such that it did not halt at merely reforming the socioeconomic structure of the island and realigning its international relations. The regime also constructed mechanisms through which the Cuban people were forced to demonstrate their loyalty, or lack thereof, to the new Communist society. As Fagen, Brody, and O'Leary point out, the authorities in effect asked, "Are you with us or against us?" Those who answered "With you" were expected to show their support for the revolution.[4] This fealty was demonstrated through personal behavior, ideological correctness, and especially overt acts of support. Such acts, performed mostly in cooperation with other revolutionaries through the regime's mass organizations, were aimed at integrating the individual into the Marxist state. Those who resisted, even passively, were viewed with suspicion and subjected to assaults, harassment, and within a short time the denial of educational and career opportunities. Hence, in a *coletilla*, or footnote, added to an antigovernment newspaper article, the government declared that for all those opposed to "totalitarian unity," there was always *paredon*, prison, exile, or contempt.[5] The government added footnotes to all newspaper articles as a means of restricting the free press on the eve of its ultimate destruction.

A component in achieving the goal of "totalitarian unity" was the enactment of programs aimed at molding the current and future generations of Cuban children along revolutionary lines. Thus, non-Communist parents had reason to fear for their children's future, as well as for their social, ideological, and spiritual well-being at the time.

The emergence of Communist youth organizations directly affected the lives and minds of children. The Pioneers, an organization for children five to thirteen years of age, was established in 1961. Holding Che Guevara as its idol, the organization's main purpose was political indoctrination and integration into the new Communist society. The following year, the Union of Young Communists was formed for youths between fourteen and twenty-seven years of age. Although membership was not compulsory in either organization, the pressure to join was enormous because members of the youth organizations received preferential treatment in all sectors of national life. Furthermore, failure to attach oneself to a Communist youth organization was deemed counterrevolutionary. Young people in such a situation and their families were subjected to the pressures and harassment mentioned earlier. James Baker, a witness to the fanaticism that characterized youth organizations, remembered, "They would march these children up and down the streets and they would say 'Who is your leader?' 'Fidel!' [children's response]. 'Who is your hero?' 'Fidel!' 'Who is your God?' 'Fidel!'. . . that was enough [to motivate parents to send their children away from Cuba].[6]

As in most totalitarian takeovers, the cult of the leader was strong in Cuba. Such scenes as Baker described, accompanied by the overall mistreatment of nonrevolutionaries, became commonplace in the new Cuba. Parents who believed Fidel Castro to be the devil incarnate preferred to send their children into exile.

In a bold move designed to bring the next generation in sync with revolutionary values, Castro declared 1961 the Year of Education. As part of that effort, the Castro regime in April closed all public and private schools for a period of eight months, while the island's education system was restructured to meet the needs of the revolution. They were also closed to supply soldiers—the children free from school—for a massive literacy campaign. Given that the regime had painted Catholic and other private schools as centers of counterrevolution and that the schools educated the children of virtually all middle- and upper-class parents, it was clear that they would not reopen. Most of the Catholic orders and other groups that had operated private schools went into exile. For many parents, the private schools had represented the last bastions against what they considered the state's ideological assault upon their children. Such was their opposition to closing the private schools that rioting erupted, especially in the cities of Santiago and Guantanamo.

Predictably, the new Cuban school system, in which attendance was compulsory, served as ideological training centers to foster atheism, veneration of Castro and the revolution, commitment to Communism, and creation of the revolution's "New Man." Faced with such a prospect, many nonrevolutionary parents were pushed into getting their children out of Cuba. Some children, such as Teresa Ponte, were kept home from school when the regime opened its new school system. She recalled how she spent the 1962 academic year, hidden from the authorities: "So that I wouldn't be a truant, so that no one would see me in the streets at ten o'clock in the morning and wonder 'What are you doing?' we were kept in the house, and the grandfather of one of my little pals in the neighborhood used to teach us. He had like a little school . . . for his grandchildren. At the time there were five of them and myself."

She also recalled the day the Catholic school she had attended was shut down and how the actions of the nuns there may have assisted her later truancy:

> The school I attended had a deal with certain parents, apparently, that whenever they [the nuns] knew they were going to be intervened [the school was to be shut down and confiscated], they were going to call the parents, and their parents would come and get their kids out of there. And that's exactly what happened. One fine day all the parents showed up to take the kids home in the middle of the day. . . . I assume that what the nuns did was burn the records. . . . There was a difficult way [the nuns thus made it hard] to trace the students to see that they were enrolled then in the public school system.[7]

The massive literacy campaign of 1961 also had important implications for parents who feared Communist indoctrination of their children. Aimed at improving Cuba's 76.4 percent literacy rate (then the fourth-highest in Latin America), the campaign called for close participation by the population—especially schoolchildren, then freed up during the closure of Cuba's schools. Although there was enthusiasm for the campaign among a broad sector of the population, there was also great social pressure for educated children to participate as "volunteers." In fact, 87.5 percent of the literacy "volunteers" were under twenty years of age. Forty percent were under fifteen.[8]

Nonrevolutionary parents had reason to be suspicious of the campaign, which took children from their homes, gave them two weeks of instruction by adult volunteers, and then sent them into the countryside to live with peasant families and teach under the auspices of a regular teacher. In this, many parents saw little more than an attempt by the regime to separate their children from them and catechize the youngsters in Communism. The revolutionary spirit that characterized the campaign only compounded their fears. The value of universal literacy is of course questionable in a society that practices the strictest form of censorship.

Nonrevolutionary parents were justified in their fears of the literacy campaign. As Lowry Nelson pointed out in his work *Cuba: The Measure of a Revolution*, the literacy campaign, while not solely politically motivated, was a socially integrating experience. Its impact, moreover, was far-reaching. It represented the first great mobilization of the whole population, of the type that would characterize Communist Cuba for years to come.[9] The teaching materials used in the campaign further revealed its blatant political purposes. For instance, in the glossary of *Venceremos* (one of the manuals used in the campaign), among the words beginning with *B* appeared *Bloqueo Economico:* "state of siege imposed by imperialism [which] . . . we have conquered thanks to the countries which trade with us."[10] The manual was also riddled with slogans such as "Friends and Enemies," "The Revolution wins all battles," and "International Unity." It was not that nonrevolutionary parents were opposed to societal goals such as universal literacy—in fact many middle-class people were teachers—but rather to the manner in which it was carried out. That their children would be pressured into separation from their families and put under the care of revolutionaries for several weeks seemed to many an ideological divide-and-conquer strategy being employed by the regime.

In addition to the very real reasons why nonrevolutionary parents feared for their children, a number of wild rumors that began circulating in 1961 heightened their fears. In light of the rapid and dramatic changes in Cuba, many believed those stories. First of all came allegations that the regime was kidnapping children and sending them to Russia for indoctrination on state farms. Given the hysterical state of mind in which many parents found themselves, some chose to send their children away from Cuba.

Another rumor concerned *patria potestad*, a term that means parental custody. The panic it caused, which first appeared in late 1960 and resurfaced periodically until 1962, was the result of a disinformation campaign carried out by the anti-Castro underground with the compliance of a Havana printer. The conspirators circulated a document they claimed was a soon-to-be announced government decree detailing a Castro regime plan to strip parents of patria potestad and transfer it to the state when a child turned three years of age. At that point, the children would be placed in state-run nurseries. They would live in dormitories and would be allowed to visit their parents at least two days a month. Those over ten years of age would be sent to the "most appropriate place," perhaps permanently.[11]

Castro declared the supposed decree a forgery. Although no evidence suggests that the regime was considering such a plan, it nevertheless produced a good amount of hysteria among some parents. Considering what they had witnessed, the stripping of patria potestad by the Cuban government seemed conceivable as a logical next step. A story of questionable validity coming out of Cuba in 1961 told of fifty mothers in the city of Bayamo who had signed a pact vowing to kill their children before handing them to Castro.[12]

Stripping parents of custody, regardless of the decree's authenticity, represented the common denominator of all parental fears: a state attempt to separate children from their families and convert them into loyal followers of the revolution. Juan Clark, a Cuban American sociologist, believed that the parents' fears were justified: "All the fears and so forth that were, you might say, disseminated there within the Cuban population . . . made them [parents] fearful they would lose patria potestad. Although it never materialized in the way it was presented in the rumor going on there . . . it did materialize in a rather indirect way through the complete closing of the private school system and then the increasing indoctrination and control and separation [of parents and children] that took place."[13]

Clark went to the real center of the issue: Patria potestad was in fact taken away indirectly. The closing of private schools and compulsory attendance in state-run schools were major factors, as was the pressure to join Communist youth organizations. Those institutions were geared, as noted earlier, to instilling revolutionary values in the next generation. In the years after Castro's consolidation of power, children who were reluctant to exhibit revolutionary enthusiasm or who engaged in subversive activities—such as failing to join a Communist youth organization, possessing religious beliefs, showing a lack of enthusiasm for the revolution and its leader, or having parents with a low level of revolutionary integration—could expect that the fact would be noted on their academic dossiers. Such sins against the revolution were used to keep those students from receiving academic awards and attending college. Similar dossiers were also kept on adults through the workplace and the local Committee for the Defense of the Revolution (CDR), the regime's watchdogs who were organized into block-by-block vigilance groups.

The separation Clark referred to was likewise significant in future years. Although the regime could not afford to destroy the family completely, it deliberately weakened it in important ways. Husbands and wives, for instance, were often called to places far away from home to engage in "volunteer" projects. Reluctance to do so, especially for the husbands, could have meant two years or more in a forced labor camp.[14] Schoolchildren were also eventually required to complete a certain amount of work in agricultural fields every year, thus separating them from their families.

In summation, it became impossible and virtually illegal for parents to prevent their children's indoctrination in Communist ideology. There was simply no shelter from the state and its doctrine. As Juan Clark pointed out, the entire institutional system on the island became a "repressive apparatus."[15] Given what Cuba's middle class believed, sending their children to the United States when they were presented with the means seemed rational. When the choice became losing their children permanently to Communism or temporarily to friends, relatives, or a religious organization in the United States, the parents of 14,048 children chose the latter. Thousands more would have liked similar opportunities.

Separation from their children was understandably difficult for most parents, especially given the disturbing reasons for the separation. Furthermore, revolutionaries in Cuba generally harassed, verbally or by other means, the relatives of those who had left in exile, and families who had sent away their children were not spared their wrath. Father Walsh commented that for Cuban families to send their children to the United States was like "nailing an American flag to their door."[16]

The parents of Pedro Pan's 14,048 children had a number of reasons for not leaving Cuba along with their offspring. In the first place, some parents were involved in underground activities on the island. Others still owned some property or businesses that they felt would be confiscated if they left. A number had relatives in political prisons or infirm parents or spouses whom they could not bear to leave behind. A large percentage could not leave with their children because they had not been able to gather the proper documentation to exit Cuba. Thanks to Operation Pedro Pan, their children were able to secure such documents more easily, and once in the United States, they could expedite the process of securing exit documents for the parents. Another important factor behind the parents' decisions was their belief that the separation from their children would be brief. Despite sincere suspicions of an impending doom, many convinced themselves that they were simply sending their children abroad to attend school for a few months and that when the Castro regime fell, they would be reunited with their children at Havana's airport. Sending children away to school was not unusual. For generations many Cuban parents, especially those of the middle and upper classes, had sent their children to boarding schools both in Cuba and abroad. Sadly, when the Castro regime remained in power and the Cuban missile crisis of October 1962 ended commercial flights between Cuba and the United States, the hoped-for short separation became several years for thousands of families.

At any rate, the arrival of unaccompanied Cuban children in South Florida beginning in late 1960 only compounded the problems faced by anxious local residents. Given the thousands of Cuban refugee families already in the area, frenzied Miamians were grappling with a refugee crisis.

Two

Operation Pedro Pan:
A Miami Priest Teams Up
with a Havana Headmaster

The enormity of the task slowly dawned on me.
Father Bryan O. Walsh

By the end of 1960, there were already around 60,000 Cuban exiles in the United States. The majority of them had fled the island after the Castro regime began its drastic turn to the left in mid-1960. Most were destitute because of restrictions imposed at that time upon what a person could take when leaving the island. A disproportionate number of refugees chose Miami, in Dade County, Florida, as their place of exile, as it was the most convenient port of entry and close to Cuba. It was also a place with which many were already familiar.

The influx of such a massive wave of needy refugees in so short a time span overwhelmed Miami's small, underfunded social service agencies. Despite those organizations' troubles in late 1960, it was clear the number of refugees would continue to skyrocket. Their difficulties became even more acute when it was discovered that some of the immigrants were unaccompanied children.

Soon to be thrust into the dilemma presented by the arrival of unaccompanied Cuban children was the young Irish-born priest Bryan Walsh. When

Walsh left his home in Limerick to pursue his studies for the priesthood, there were doubts about his chances for success. One of five children from a prosperous family, the six-foot, four-inch, athletically built Walsh had a severe speech impediment that many felt would hinder his dream of working as a missionary in Africa. Despite his difficulty Walsh graduated from St. Mary's Seminary in Baltimore in 1954, and the young priest decided to stay in the United States, where he would not have to speak a foreign language. He commented, "I figured, if they had trouble understanding me in English, how would they ever understand me in Swahili?" His speech impediment mysteriously disappeared weeks after his ordination while delivering his first sermon.

Initially assigned to a parish in Central Florida, Walsh was transferred to the Diocese of Miami in January 1957.[1] There he became the director of the Catholic Welfare Bureau, a "small, licensed child caring and adoption agency, then caring for about eighty children."[2] His ability to meet challenges throughout his career would be put to the first real test in 1960, in ways he had probably never imagined.

Walsh's involvement with unaccompanied Cuban children began in November 1960, when he was introduced to fifteen-year-old Pedro Menendez in his office at the Catholic Welfare Bureau. Attempting to keep Pedro out of political trouble at home and to prevent his indoctrination into Communism in Cuba, his parents had sent him to Miami by himself. Pedro's parents expected the boy to be cared for by relatives and friends already in exile, but because of their own destitution, the families in Miami passed Pedro from one to another until the youngster finally became homeless. When he was brought to Father Walsh a month later, the boy had lost twenty pounds. The priest remembered, "It was a scared and hungry child that stood in my office that November afternoon."[3]

Walsh realized that his encounter with Pedro Menendez was only the beginning of a local child welfare problem that was certain to grow in the coming months. As director of the Catholic Welfare Bureau, he was directly concerned with the issue of dependent children in Miami. Having witnessed the explosion of cases at other social service agencies in the area firsthand, and expecting the same in his agency, Walsh immediately began contemplating how to deal with the anticipated crisis. Also alerting Walsh was an incident in Key West, Florida, where a Cuban woman had appeared before a judge in juvenile court and asked him to find suitable temporary homes for her children. She explained that she had smuggled them out of Cuba so that she could rejoin her husband in counterrevolutionary activities.[4]

By the time Walsh met Pedro Menendez, local leaders in Miami had become anxious about the complications of the Cuban influx. Believing the refugee problem was a national concern, local leaders thought it was the federal government's responsibility to take effective action. Hence, local citizens created the Cuban Refugee Executive Committee to solicit help from Washington, D.C. In November 1960 the committee formally petitioned President Dwight D. Eisenhower for assistance in employment, social services, counseling services, and the determination of immigration status for the refugees.[5] Most of all, the group wanted the refugees relocated elsewhere in the country. In response, Eisenhower sent Tracy Voorhees to Miami as his special representative to study the situation and to work with the Cuban Refugee Executive Committee. As the former head of the Hungarian Refugee Program in Camp Kilmer, New Jersey, Voorhees seemed the logical choice.

Walsh took advantage of the Voorhees mission to press his concern about the crisis he expected in the arrival of unaccompanied Cuban children. During the third week of November, the priest addressed representatives of Dade County's child welfare agencies during a meeting called at his request by the Child Care Division of Miami's Welfare Planning Council, the "community agency charged with the responsibility for identifying needs and planning for solutions in the social welfare field."[6] At the meeting Walsh unveiled his plan to provide care for unaccompanied Cuban children, whose numbers he believed would increase dramatically in the near future. Walsh said he thought proper care could be provided only through federal funding, which should be channeled to local, private, religious child care agencies, which would provide the actual care.[7]

Walsh had good reasons for wanting private, religious agencies to provide the services themselves, using federal funds. He believed it was important to Cuban parents that their children's religious heritage be protected. Furthermore, the Hungarian program that Voorhees had coordinated in 1956 had placed many minors in foster care without what Walsh called the "usual investigation and planning regarded as essential by child welfare agencies."[8] The groups that Voorhees had used were unprepared to carry out such a project. To Walsh's dismay, Voorhees had already contacted those same unfit agencies to handle Cuban relocation, and Walsh feared a repeat of the 1956 child care disaster if Voorhees was not presented with an alternative.

The Welfare Planning Council accepted Walsh's idea and forwarded it to the Cuban Refugee Executive Committee, which in turn agreed to present it to Voorhees. In keeping with their religious concerns, three local agencies—Walsh's Catholic Welfare Bureau, the Jewish Family and Children's Service, and the Children's Service Bureau (Protestant, non-denominational)—offered to provide care within the children's religious heritage.[9]

After reviewing the situation in Miami, Voorhees delivered his report to President Eisenhower. The administration agreed to provide $1 million from the president's contingency fund under the Mutual Security Act to help alleviate the situation, and the Cuban Refugee Emergency Center opened its doors in Miami during the first week of December 1960. Services to Cuban refugees ranged from medical care to resettlement. Four long-established volunteer refugee relief agencies were utilized: the National Catholic Welfare Conference, the International Rescue Commission, the Church World Service, and the United Hebrew Immigrant Aid Society (United HIAS). On the part of the Welfare Planning Council, Voorhees's request called for part of the money to be used for assisting Cuban refugee children "in extreme need," but only after the problem of dependent Cuban minors proved "beyond what private charity could do."[10]

Thus the federal government responded to the Miami area's cry for help. For his part, Walsh at least received the promise of federal funds if the problem of dependent children became serious. Such a contingency would not take long.

While Walsh prepared for the anticipated crisis in Miami, a group of Cuban anti-Castro underground operatives were likewise planning for the protection of Cuban children. In the middle of this effort was James Baker, the headmaster of Ruston Academy in Havana. Ruston Academy was founded in 1920 by the American educator Aaron Ruston and his sister. Their dream of establishing an American school in Cuba was realized by a combination of hard work and the investment of their life savings. By the 1930s, Ruston Academy had achieved a high standing among Cuban schools, and its student body was drawn primarily from wealthy Americans living in Cuba and from the native-born elite.

James Baker went to Ruston Academy as an English teacher in 1930. An appealing man with a trace of an accent from his native Kentucky, Baker began his Ruston career armed with a Harvard education. He left Ruston in 1936 but returned in 1944 to take over the school's administration when Aaron Ruston fell ill. Ruston died in 1949, followed soon afterward by his sister. Baker and his wife, Sybil, inherited the school and established Ruston Academy as the first private nonprofit educational foundation in Cuba.

The Bakers and their children were among the "American Cubans." Although retaining U.S. citizenship, the Bakers and other Americans on the island developed strong emotional ties with Cuba and considered it an adopted homeland. When the Batista dictatorship was deposed in January 1959, James Baker shared in the national euphoria, calling it "the most exciting time in my life."[11] Through his Ruston Academy family, Baker was closely acquainted with various ministers in the new government during the regime's first few months in power. By May 1959, though, Baker had become disillusioned with the revolution and was desperately searching for something about the regime in which to believe. Later that year, Baker had become so thoroughly discontented by Fidel Castro's dictatorial manner and his appointment of Communists to key positions in government that Baker joined the clandestine effort to oust him.[12]

In November 1960 Baker began organizing a covert effort to place around two hundred children of underground operatives out of the Castro regime's reach. During the second week of December, Baker traveled to Miami to make the preliminary arrangements. He hoped the trip would also help Cuban parents who were not in the underground but wanted to get their children out of Cuba. In any case, Baker's mission marked the first deliberate effort to take children out of Castro's Cuba and bring them to the United States in a planned, systematic fashion.

Baker's purpose in Miami was twofold. First, he solicited financial assistance from the heads of American companies formerly in Cuba, which were waiting to return, for his plan to bring the children from Cuba and provide for their care once they arrived. Second, after the businessmen agreed to provide the money, Baker began searching for a suitable place to establish a temporary boarding school. While he was working out the details for his school, someone suggested that he speak to Father Walsh, and the headmaster agreed to do so.

During their crucial meeting, Walsh persuaded Baker to drop his idea of establishing a boarding school for the children he hoped to bring to Miami. Walsh informed the headmaster of the promised federal funds for unaccompanied Cuban children and of the plan for their care. The priest explained that "uncoordinated and scattered efforts" would only hurt the cause of helping unaccompanied Cuban children.[13] He further explained that only licensed child-placing agencies should be used and that only a social agency could plan for the child's total care, including questions of custody. He also pointed out the benefits of foster care over institutional care and the importance to the Cuban parents of safeguarding their children's religious heritage while under another's care.

Baker was impressed by Walsh's competence. Even more important, the priest had solved the problem of caring for the children—no doubt one of the greatest challenges Baker would have faced. Baker recalled his meeting with Walsh: "I would emphasize the major importance of Father Walsh in all this. . . . He was the director of the Catholic Welfare Bureau. He had no authority. He did not have the prestige that he had ten or fifteen years later. . . . It was the result of his foresight, his awareness of what was happening . . . and his strong desire to do something to find a solution. When I went to see him in December of 1960, he had already talked to some people [in the federal government]."[14]

When the two men agreed to work together, Walsh's volunteering to see to the children's care solved half of Baker's problem. Now the headmaster had to worry only about getting the children out of Cuba—an effort soon to be nicknamed Operation Pedro Pan. Walsh's responsibility was to provide care as soon as they arrived at Miami International Airport (MIA).

Until he met Baker, Walsh was simply planning to assist Cuban children in Miami who were brought to his attention. He assumed the children he would help would be staying with relatives or friends in Miami who, as in the case of Pedro Menendez, could no longer care for them. In working with Baker, Walsh greatly expanded his role. His agency had now committed itself to the responsibility of both receiving and providing immediate care for unaccompanied Cuban children at the point of entry, Miami International Airport. Within a few weeks Walsh would become even more deeply involved in the plan's Pedro Pan component, and over the next twenty-two months Baker's original estimate of two hundred children would swell to more than 14,000.

Immediately after the Walsh-Baker meeting, a system was devised to bring the children to the United States, first by providing the youngsters with student visas from the U.S. Embassy in Havana. The embassy required proof of enrollment in an American school and a guarantee that an acceptable individual or agency would be responsible for the "students" while in the United States. To meet the latter requirement, Walsh gave Baker a letter for the embassy in Havana, accepting full responsibility for any minor the headmaster designated. To supply proof of enrollment, Baker would send Walsh lists of children's names that Walsh would pass to former Havana resident Norma Lemberg, who would receive the numbers requested of U.S. Immigration Form I-20 (required proof of enrollment) from Agnes Elward at Coral Gables High School in Dade County. Walsh would send the forms to Baker in Cuba, who would give them to the children's parents. At that point, the children would be put aboard one of the daily flights to Miami, where Walsh would meet them. Payment for the airfare would come from the businessmen Baker had met with earlier in Miami.[15] So that the Cuban government could not trace the source of the funds, the American corporate leaders, aided by some British companies, would issue checks to the Catholic Welfare Bureau, which in turn issued checks to carefully selected U.S. citizens in Miami. Those citizens then sent personal checks for the airfare to the W. Henry Smith Agency, an American-owned travel agency still operating in Havana.

Baker returned to Havana on December 13 to activate the plan. Fearing that the Cuban government would clamp down if it learned of a children's exodus, he and Walsh agreed to maintain secrecy and communicate only via the U.S. diplomatic pouch, an arrangement possible with the cooperation of the State Department. Before leaving Miami, Baker took the required paperwork for around twenty-five children whose parents had specifically asked him for help.[16] Only two days after Baker's departure, Walsh received a list from Havana of the first 125 children's names.[17]

Walsh spent much of his time between Baker's departure and Christmas searching for temporary facilities to house the children. Uncertainty about the exact time of the children's arrival and about whether they would arrive as a group was his greatest dilemma. If only a few showed up before January, he reasoned, the situation could be easily managed. Yet, a likely scenario was that all the children would show up within days of one another, as it was rumored that the Castro government was preparing to announce a decree on January 1, 1961, prohibiting the departure of children from Cuba.

Walsh received a call on Christmas Eve informing him that some of the children might be arriving the next day. The young priest had been preparing sites for the children, but unfortunately the accommodations were still a couple of weeks away from being ready. In any case, he had to prepare for an immediate and maximum arrival.

That very afternoon, a solution came to Walsh:

As I drove home, the faith with which I had made the promise to James Baker was justified and God gave me a solution to the immediate problem, the first of many such answers to prayer in the months and years to come. My way home took me by Assumption Academy, a private girls' boarding school run by the Sisters of the Assumption. I had never been in the place, but I realized suddenly that the school would be empty for the holidays and that about 200 children could be accommodated there, even if they all came on the same flight. I stopped and went in to make my plea. Mother Elizabeth was most responsive and agreed to allow us to use the school, providing everyone could be out by the sixth of January. I remember her remarking that she could not refuse such a request on Christmas Eve. She did not realize that many would be teenage boys and I did not tell her.[18]

Walsh was also able to fall back on the Catholic Welfare Bureau's facilities at St. Joseph's Villa. That institution, run by the Sisters of St. Joseph, had around twenty children in residence and nine empty beds. Walsh worked it out so that at least ten to twelve boys could stay there overnight.

On Christmas morning, Walsh asked Louise Cooper, a social worker with the Catholic Welfare Bureau, to accompany him to the airport to meet the two flights from Cuba. He wrote of his feelings during those intense hours: "By this time we ourselves had become emotionally involved in the race against the January 1st deadline. No longer were we simply a social agency concerned about a community problem. We were now sharing the worries of families we did not even know, hundreds of miles away in a life and death struggle in the Cold War. Our excitement rose as time drew near for the first of the flights to arrive."[19]

Anticlimactically, the airplane contained no unaccompanied children. The day was not wasted, though, as Walsh devised cooperative work arrangements with Immigration and Naturalization Service officials at Miami International Airport. In later years, he complimented INS official Patrick Crowley and his staff for their cooperation over the next twenty-two months.[20]

The following day, December 26, Walsh received several requests to place Cuban children already in Miami who had been staying with relatives and friends. Some of them were on Baker's list but had been sent instead with tourist visas by parents not willing to risk waiting until January 1, 1961. Sending children on tourist visas seemed risky, as parents could not be certain that their children would be cared for unless they officially arrived as students. In any case, the children had not been met at the airport by the Catholic Welfare Bureau because Walsh had no advance notice of their arrival. Instead of taking those children under care immediately on December 26, he waited briefly, until an unaccompanied child was met at the airport, before officially beginning the program.

That afternoon, December 26, on the last flight from Havana, the first children arrived seeking out Father Walsh—a brother and sister, Sixto and Vivian Aquino. The plan devised two weeks earlier was by all indications in motion and Operation Pedro Pan was under way. The two children were immediately taken under the care of Walsh's agency, thus marking the birth of the Cuban Children's Program, which also assumed the care of the children whose guardians had contacted Walsh earlier. By December 31 Walsh had met twenty-two additional children at the airport and had taken over their care.

On December 29 Walsh concluded that the number of refugee children had reached a point beyond the capacity of private charity. He formally requested the money Voorhees had promised. There was a transmittal delay because the U.S. government had never actually funded foster care for refugee children. It was not until February 1961 that the money was finally channeled to the Cuban Children's Program through the national resettlement agencies cooperating with the Cuban Refugee Emergency Center.[21]

Strangely, all of the children had arrived with regular tourist visas. Although Walsh took in all children who needed care despite documentation, it puzzled him that none had been able to obtain student visas. The mystery was solved on December 30, when Walsh received a telephone call from James Baker (despite their agreement not to communicate in that fashion). Baker explained that the U.S. Embassy in Havana was holding up the issuance of student visas, and he instructed Walsh to contact Frank Auerbach of the Visa Section of the Department of State in Washington, D.C. Walsh did so that day.

In their December 30 conversation, Auerbach explained to Walsh that the U.S. government would grant the children student visas only if a nongovernment organization assumed "ultimate" responsibility for the children. Apparently Auerbach wanted more than the letter Walsh had sent to the embassy two weeks earlier. After all, it was obvious that the reason for the children's journey was more than education. In response, the young Walsh, low in the church hierarchy, made a bold decision, based on the possibility that Castro would cut off emigration within two days. He sent the required notarized statement to the State Department via special delivery on his own authority, without consulting his ecclesiastical superiors in the Diocese of Miami. He was prepared to accept the consequences. Walsh later described what happened when Bishop Carroll learned of his action: "One day I came back to my apartment and the archbishop was calling. 'Where have you been? I've been trying to call you all day.' So I said, 'I've been doing your work. What's up?' He said, 'This fellow from the State Department [Auerbach] has been trying to call you, and somehow or another he got hold of me. . . . He wants to talk to you about some children from Cuba.' I said, 'Oh, yes, I know what it's about.'"[22]

Walsh was feeling consternation. As far as the young priest was concerned, the bishop, who was apparently difficult to work with, might view the situation in any number of ways. Walsh recalled the rest of the phone conversation:

So here I am [thinking] in the back of my mind, How am I going to tell him I went out on this limb? Well, my career is finished but it's worth it for two hundred kids. So when Carroll said, "He [Auerbach] said something about two hundred kids," I said, "Oh, yes, Archbishop, that's right." He said, "Are you limiting? Did you put that limit of two hundred?" I said, "No, no, Archbishop." It was the fastest thing the guy ever did. I said, "I'm not putting any limit on the number of children. There's just two hundred on the first list." He said, "That's right, take all the kids! Take everyone! Don't be restricting them. You're always restricting! You're always saying no!" It was the exact opposite of what I was going to try to explain to him . . . and here he was accusing me of being too restrictive instead of too generous! . . . It got me off the hook entirely.[23]

Walsh now at least had the comfort of the diocese's backing.

New Year's Day, 1961, came and went with no announcement from Castro about the emigration of children. Even so, the dictator ordered the U.S. Embassy in Havana to cut its staff to fifteen persons, correctly charging that it was the hub of counterrevolutionary activity. Two days later President Eisenhower severed all diplomatic relations with Cuba. Next came the mutual closing of embassies and consulates. Cubans were now denied conventional channels of receiving proper documents to enter the United States, including student visas. It seemed to Father Walsh and those working with him in Miami that Operation Pedro Pan had come to an abrupt end.

James Baker left Cuba on January 5 when the embassy closed. Baker had been able to secure student visas only for the twenty to twenty-five children whose names he had taken to Miami a few weeks earlier, having brought the required paperwork back to Havana himself. Yet, unlike his collaborators in Florida, Baker knew the operation would continue.[24]

Three

International Intrigue:
Working Out the Logistics

Somehow the weather, the day, the time, and the happenings of the past week all combined to create an atmosphere of intrigue and conspiracy.
Bryan O. Walsh

In anticipation of his January 5 departure, James Baker had formed a secret committee in Havana equipped with the means to continue the children's exodus. The headmaster revealed his committee's plan to Father Walsh and Louise Cooper during a January 6 meeting in Miami. He explained how, through their diplomatic connections, his Havana committee could secure British student visas for the children to travel to Kingston, Jamaica. The committee's contacts at the Dutch Embassy could then arrange for the children to travel from Cuba aboard KLM Royal Dutch Airlines on its direct weekly flight from Havana to Kingston. The Cuban children aboard that flight who were being rescued would receive their U.S. visas in Kingston and travel to Miami the following day. The other weekly KLM flight from Havana to Kingston made a stopover in Miami. Children on that flight who left Cuba with visas for Jamaica would then simply disembark in Miami. Success of the plan would require the cooperation of the U.S. and British governments.[1]

Walsh, Baker, and Cooper decided immediately to call Frank Auerbach in the State Department, who expressed interest in the Jamaica plan. Auerbach invited Walsh to call on him when the young priest arrived in Washington on Sunday, January 8, for a White House Conference on the Aging.[2]

After arriving in Washington, Walsh took a taxi to the State Department building for his 2:00 p.m. appointment with Auerbach, waiting at the pre-arranged site by a side entrance. Recalling his mood that Sunday afternoon, Walsh wrote, "It was a bright, cold winter afternoon, and the streets around the State Department were completely deserted. Somehow, the weather, the day, the time, the happenings of the past weeks all combined to create an atmosphere of intrigue and conspiracy. Promptly at two, Mr. Auerbach drove up and we met for the first time."[3]

They held their meeting in the State Department building, along with Robert F. Hale, director of the Visa Office. For three hours, Walsh, Auerbach, and Hale discussed the available channels for continuing Operation Pedro Pan. Baker's Jamaica plan would overcome the technical difficulties posed by the break in U.S.-Cuban diplomatic relations, as the children would leave Cuba with visas granted by the British Embassy. Nevertheless, Walsh no doubt wanted assurances that the State Department could arrange for the children who arrived in Jamaica to receive their U.S. visas immediately upon their arrival. Hale and Auerbach were agreeable to the priest's request but, in spite of the Baker committee's connections and their own support, cooperation from the British government would have to come from a level higher than that of the diplomats stationed in Havana.[4]

The three men also discussed the possibility of arranging for the children to travel directly to the United States by granting them visa waivers—that is, the waiving of visa requirements by the U.S. government, pursuant to section 212 (d) (4) (A) of the Immigration and Nationality Act. Requests for visa waivers could officially be made by letter, telegram, telephone call, or personal visit. Supporting information came from relatives, friends, employers, members of Congress, officers of voluntary agencies, and other interested persons. To justify visa waivers, the State Department reserved their use for emergency situations.[5]

Auerbach suggested that Walsh's Catholic Welfare Bureau petition the State Department for visa waivers for the Cuban children, justified by the threat of Communist indoctrination.[6] With visa waiver documents in hand, children could fly directly on regular commercial flights between Havana and Miami—thus minimizing the use of the more complex Jamaica channel.

The three men also reaffirmed that, for the moment, responsibility for the children would remain with Walsh's agency. (In a short time the Catholic Welfare Bureau's role became more formalized and included other voluntary organizations.) At that point, only three problems persisted in terms of visa waivers. First was the question of whether the Department of Justice would allow immigration to be conducted in that fashion. Second, would Cuban officials accept visa waivers as proper documentation? Finally, by what means would the children in Cuba receive the waivers? In any case, the men decided that both the Jamaica and visa waiver projects, if approved, had to remain secret. They believed that if the Castro regime discovered a U.S.-backed children's exodus, it would be stopped immediately.

Walsh spent the next day, January 9, 1961, in telephoning from Washington, D.C. He first called Father William Connolly, the chancellor of the Diocese of Kingston. He discussed the possibility of the diocese helping Cuban children during their brief stay in Jamaica while awaiting U.S. visas. Connolly believed they could help but would first have to get permission from his bishop. Walsh then called his office in Miami to arrange a trip to Jamaica.[7]

The same day, British officials were briefed on the Jamaica plan and asked for help. Later that day, Walsh learned of the United Kingdom's willingness to grant the necessary visas for the children to travel to Jamaica. All that remained was to put the Jamaica plan into action. In other good news for Walsh that day, the U.S. Department of Justice approved the State Department's request to grant the children visa waivers. In fact, Walsh was given blanket authority to issue waivers, typed on Catholic Welfare Bureau letterhead, to any child from six to sixteen years of age.[8] Walsh could grant waivers also to sixteen- to eighteen-year-olds after the State Department had checked their names for security clearances. The security checks were made against the State Department's "lookout book" and against 250,000 case records in the Havana and Santiago files that had been transferred from Cuba to the Visa Office.[9]

For Cubans over eighteen, a visa waiver would have to be requested by a "first degree relative" in the United States.[10] In such a case, a Cuban child who was admitted to the United States under a visa waiver from Father Walsh could then apply for a waiver for his or her parents.

As for immigration status, nearly all the children, as well as 89 percent of all the period's Cuban refugees, were granted "parole" status by U.S. immigration officials.[11] Their type of parole status authorized "indefinite voluntary departure," thus protecting the refugees from deportation proceedings.[12] However, they could not apply for U.S. citizenship unless they traveled abroad and applied for an immigrant visa.[13] In 1966, when it was clear that Cuban exiles' stay in the United States would be prolonged, that restriction was lifted, thanks to Walsh's key role in the passage of the Cuban Adjustment Act. Walsh argued that the first system discriminated against those who lacked the financial resources to travel abroad. The Adjustment Act required a refugee to stay only one year and one day in the United States before applying for resident status.[14]

In January 1961, upon learning of the Jamaica plan's approval, James Baker contacted his Havana committee and gave them the go-ahead to approach their contacts at the British Embassy. Father Walsh, by then having abandoned the White House conference, flew to Kingston the next day with Rachel Erwin, supervisor of child welfare for the Catholic Welfare Bureau. In Kingston, Walsh and Erwin met with Father Connolly, the U.S. consul general, and officials from KLM and Pan American Airlines. Having been alerted by the State Department earlier, the U.S. consul general had already secured the cooperation of local officials in Jamaica. Father Connolly, meanwhile, had made arrangements for the Cuban children to stay at Jamaican Catholic boarding schools while they awaited their U.S. visas, which were planned to be granted quickly. A chilling incident at Kingston's airport made Walsh realize his deep involvement in a covert, international cold war scheme. He described the event:

> Next stop on our schedule was to return to the airport to see the arrival of a KLM flight from Havana. While we were waiting, a Cuban man came up to me and asked if I was there to meet the children from Cuba. Needless to say his question was a shock, since the whole Operation Pedro Pan was supposed to be a secret and we were trying to avoid giving the Cuban authorities the impression that there was a wide-scale organized effort to help children leave the island. We were sure that this would bring about reprisals against parents and

others in Cuba who were cooperating. I tried to look innocent and told him that we were simply curious to see the flight. But by now we were beginning to feel that we were really involved in an international intrigue.[15]

Within a few days Walsh and his team of assistants began receiving Cuban children with visa waivers at Miami International Airport. On January 17 the first group of children made it to Jamaica on a nonstop flight, and the four boys and three girls arrived in Miami with their U.S. visas the following afternoon. The plans had worked. Operation Pedro Pan was once again in full swing.[16]

James Baker continued working on the program for several months after his arrival in Miami. Taking charge of airport details and meeting the daily flights from Cuba, as well as serving as a house father in one of the homes Walsh had established for Cuban boys, Baker and his family faced the same destitution as all the other refugees of the period. Like most Cubans, the Bakers were awaiting the fall of Fidel Castro so that they could return to Cuba. After turning down several lucrative job offers from international schools, Baker finally accepted a teaching position in Bogota, Colombia. He retired several years later and settled with his wife in Ormond Beach, Florida.

Those who carried out Operation Pedro Pan, as well as those whose cooperation made it possible, had a variety of motives in doing so. The project itself might be viewed on two distinct levels. The first was humanitarian, seen primarily in the actions of Father Walsh. Although partly motivated by the struggle against Communism, he believed that helping Cuban parents send their youngsters abroad was the lesser of two evils—the other being that the children might get into trouble in Cuba or become victims of Communist indoctrination.[17] The young priest, understanding the hardship of family separation, apparently held to the belief that a temporary geographical separation was preferable to a permanent ideological and spiritual division. The immense gratitude he received years later on behalf of thousands who had been Pedro Pan children indicated that he was correct.

The behavior of James Baker, while in part a response to strategic considerations, must also be viewed as humanitarian. The headmaster could have easily been arrested and imprisoned in Cuba for his actions. After all, Baker could instead have sold his property and returned safely to the United States. Yet, he did not do so because of his sincere love for his adopted homeland. When asked why he risked his life and freedom to fight Castro and help Cuban children, he responded, tearfully and choked with emotion, "I was Cuban. Cuba was home. Castro was threatening my home." He also mentioned the emotional crisis that one of his sons experienced when the family went into exile, as Cuba was the only place the youngster had ever called home.[18]

Others in the Cuban underground were likewise motivated by their concern for Cuban children and their future. Although obvious strategic motives fueled the operation during its first four months, as discussed later, many in the underground continued helping the program until its end in October 1962. There was no tangible reason for them to do so; from their point of view, it served no purpose in the effort to overthrow Castro. Furthermore, most underground operatives who assisted Operation Pedro Pan were primarily involved in other, more substantial counterrevolutionary activities. Nevertheless, because they were in a position to aid anguished parents alienated from the new society, they helped.

The ease with which Walsh, Baker, and others involved in Operation Pedro Pan were able to bring Cuban children to the United States, however, inevitably begs the question as to why the U.S. government was so accommodating. In fact, the U.S. government eventually adopted an open-arms policy for Cuban refugees by virtually relaxing immigration requirements altogether. To help the Cubans, it also financed and managed the largest refugee program in U.S. history. What, then, compelled the U.S. government to grant such benefits to Cuban refugees in general and unaccompanied Cuban children in particular? The answer, I believe, lies in the evolution of U.S. policy toward Cuba during the early 1960s.

In late 1960, the U.S. Central Intelligence Agency (CIA) was working on a scheme to overthrow the Castro regime as a clandestine part of American foreign policy. The plan envisioned an invasion of Cuba by American-trained Cuban exiles (then training in Central America), timed possibly with a coordinated underground uprising. Even though in the end the underground was not told of the day, time, or place of the invasion, planners did for some time expect the groups to play a major role in connection with the operation. As alluded to in chapter 1, many underground operatives made their participation contingent upon the safety of their children. For CIA strategists, then, the children's exodus was a preparatory gesture for what became the Bay of Pigs invasion of April 1961.[19] It was during the invasion's planning stage that Auerbach and his superiors so graciously approved Baker's Jamaica plan and even suggested the use of visa waivers. Not that Pedro Pan was limited to the children of underground operatives— in fact many who were not directly connected to clandestine anti-Castro groups were able to send their children during the early months of the program.

When the CIA's strategy failed at the Bay of Pigs, it reportedly lost interest in the children's exodus and disengaged itself from Operation Pedro Pan. Yet, the operation not only continued but blossomed into the thousands and remained open to all Cuban children whose parents wished to send them to the United States. Walsh explained that Pedro Pan's first four months, stimulated by intelligence concerns, created enough momentum to carry it through until the October missile crisis of 1962.[20] The U.S. government allowed it to continue thanks to an alteration in its policy against Castro after military options in Cuba proved futile.

People who wanted to leave Cuba during the early 1960s were primarily those who had lost their livelihoods and lifestyles in the revolution; they were, with some exceptions, middle- to upper-class Cubans, those whose skills were crucial in nation building. Facilitating their entry into the United States, it was believed, would cause a brain drain in Cuba that would ultimately bring about Castro's downfall. Since Operation Pedro Pan was already in place, sapping Cuba of a large sector of its educated class, the U.S. government allowed it to continue. Simply put, while the efforts of Walsh and others involved in Pedro Pan after April 1961 remained unselfish and benevolent, the end result was in line with U.S. policy.

The U.S. government's accommodation of Cuban refugees also served hemispheric relations. The U.S. failure to dislodge Communism from the Americas was a bitter disappointment; neglect of refugees from the country the United States had let down would have aggravated the failure. The credibility of the United States and its policy of helping other nations fight Communism within their borders would have been severely undermined. That sentiment was expressed by Robert W. Jones, the State Department's deputy undersecretary for administration, before a Senate subcommittee on refugees and escapees. Referring to Cuban refugees in the United States, Jones stated: "I want to stress the importance of [the Cuban Refugee Program] in terms of the political aspects of our foreign policy. The eyes of the people of all free governments are upon us, particularly our Central and

South American neighbors. It becomes essential therefore that our han-
dling of these victims of one of the most recent Communist manipulations
be forceful, immediate, and adequate."

He later commented on refugee programs in general:

I should like to remind this committee that, although the several
refugee programs to which the United States continues to give significant financial support could be fully justified on the basis of humanitarian motives alone, these programs are of significant economic and
political importance within the context of our overall foreign policy.
Each dollar expended to help a refugee or an escapee helps to prove
America's concern for the oppressed. It is a symbol of our sustained
interest in and concern for the subjugated peoples of the world living
under tyranny, no matter the name or form.[21]

It was also clear that the U.S. government sought to accommodate the
Cuban refugees in order to establish a firm anti-Castro base within the United
States. Besides the propaganda value of desperate refugees seeking asylum
from a Communist regime—and America's generosity toward them—the exiles could act as a force to keep alive the goal of a non-Communist Cuba. In
that scenario, the United States hoped possibly to produce and sustain a
guerrilla war against Castro. The exiles, Marxism's victims, would also supply
a political force that would buttress U.S. foreign policy by providing a re-
sounding anti-Castro and anti-Communist voice in the world community.

Thus, as the central element of strategy against the Castro regime after
April 1961, the U.S. government stimulated the exodus from Cuba by
accommodating the island's refugees; it did so through lenient immigration requirements and a program designed to help refugees adapt to life
in the United States (the Cuban Refugee Program, of which the Cuban
Children's Program ultimately became a part). The end sought by the
United States should not, however, distract from the humanitarian efforts
of Father Walsh and others on the front lines of Cuban refugee relief. Nor
should it be assumed that relief workers or the refugees themselves were
somehow manipulated by the U.S. government. The desire to leave Cuba
was strong among those who ultimately chose exile, with or without encouragement from the U.S. government. The United States simply took
advantage of the inevitable tide of people who found life under a Com-

munist regime intolerable and used them in order to try to oust that regime. The desires of the refugees were no different.

Another question of governmental motives is whether the Cuban government knew of the children's exodus; if so, why was it allowed? Although the Castro regime may have been ignorant of Pedro Pan at the very beginning, figuring out the operation would not have been difficult, given the 14,048 heart-wrenching good-byes between children and parents at Havana's high-surveillance airport over a twenty-two month period, along with the common destination of all the children. Why, then, did Castro allow the exodus of children?

First of all, Castro would have seen Operation Pedro Pan and Cuban emigration in general an efficient way to get rid of at least part of his domestic opposition. The brain drain devised by the United States was for Castro a "purification" effect. This miscalculation by the U.S. allowed Castro to consolidate his revolution much more quickly and with far greater ease.[22] The Cuban regime clamped down on emigration only years later, when the loss of skilled people began taking its toll. Emigration in later years also became a public relations embarrassment: massive numbers of people desperate to leave what Castro touted as a socioeconomic paradise.

Another possible reason for Castro's inaction is diplomatic concerns. His regime, although strengthened by its victory at the Bay of Pigs, still had a long way to go to gain international legitimacy. To impose a totalitarian policy at Cuba's international airport would certainly have had repercussions. Moreover, some key figures in the Cuban government had a personal interest in the continuation of the exodus—specifically, those who had become disillusioned and wanted to send their children (or those of relatives) out of Cuba via Pedro Pan. In one such case, a high-ranking Cuban diplomat stationed in Europe, after his children had been rescued by Operation Pedro Pan, asked for and received asylum at the nearest U.S. consulate.[23]

Operation Pedro Pan and the overall exodus from Cuba during the early 1960s were permitted because they served the immediate goals of both the Cuban and U.S. governments. Still, Operation Pedro Pan would have been impossible if not for the genuine humanitarian motives of those who carried it out, and its story remains one of kindness and sincere concern for the well-being of children.

Four

Behind the Iron Curtain:
The Operation Inside Cuba

Nothing in Cuba was safe. Everything inside Cuba could change from one day to the next.
Margarita Oteiza

After Walsh laid the groundwork for Pedro Pan in Washington, Kingston, and Miami, the Cuban underground sprung into action. Because the operation was surreptitious and somewhat decentralized in Cuba, the number of people involved in the effort will never be known. Thankfully, however, the names and stories of some of the principal figures surfaced years later in exile, and an outline of their actions became visible.

There were three principal objectives for those who executed Operation Pedro Pan on the island. First was the task of delivering the clandestinely received exit papers to the children, as acceptable documentation was required to purchase airline tickets and depart from Cuba's international airport. Second, money to purchase airline tickets had to be procured for Cuban parents who lacked either funds or someone in exile to help them. That component of the operation was particularly challenging because at one point the Cuban government, while outlawing the use of U.S. dollars in Cuba, required that airline tickets be purchased with money orders paid for in U.S. currency. Last, because so many Cubans were frantically trying to leave Cuba, seats were scarce aboard flights to the United States. Due to the limited amount of space, many children with visas or visa waivers were unable to leave Cuba before Operation Pedro Pan ended in October 1962.

For his part, Walsh needed to send only a small number of visa waivers to Cuba, as it was discovered early on that Cuban officials would accept a waiver that bore only a copy of his signature. Thus, the priest sent only twelve or so of the documents to the island—blank in all spaces except for his signature. In Cuba, underground printers reproduced them in great quantities for distribution. The only names that Walsh sent to Cuba or that were given to him by messengers were those of children between sixteen and eighteen who needed security clearance from the State Department.[1]

In Operation Pedro Pan's earliest stages, besides the children of underground operatives, a disproportionate number of children came from Cuba's Catholic schools. When it became obvious that the schools were to be shut down, a strong signal to parents about the Castro regime's redirection, visa waivers were delivered en masse to those institutions. The priests, brothers, and nuns then distributed the documents to their students' parents. Also included at this stage were children of families closely connected to the church in other ways, as well as those in Cuba's many non-Catholic private schools.[2] The role of the Roman Catholic hierarchy in Cuba, particularly that of Cardinal Arteaga, was reportedly significant in that effort.[3] After Operation Pedro Pan's initial stages, a broader segment of the population took advantage of the program.

Secret underground networks that extended to every corner of Cuba likewise distributed exit papers to children. For the most part, the networks were already in place for other covert activities. Usually it was the heads of those networks in Havana who had primary access to the documents. In any case, requests for exit papers could be made at any point in the network. A parent seeking to send a child to the United States would probably have contacted a member of the clergy or a former local politician, who could make the request for exit papers to a network operative. From there, the request worked its way up the network to its head, who then produced a visa waiver and, if necessary, an airline ticket. Less frequently, a child's passport worked its way up the network, and the chief secured a regular, or sometimes phony, visa. In either case the proper documentation then wound its way back down to the child's parents.

In the case of visa waivers specifically, lists of children's names often found their way through the network. In those instances, the waivers were filled out and sent, complete with Walsh's reproduced signature, to the child's parents. In other cases the network head received only a number of waiver requests, which were supplied by way of forms that were blank except for the copied signature. It was believed that lists of names would have gotten the bearers into trouble if they were searched. In either case, supplies of visa waivers were frequently kept in embassies with the cooperation of foreign diplomatic officials. Foreign embassies were also used for producing phony visas, as they were safe from sudden police raids. The most supportive seem to have been the Panamanian, British, and Italian embassies. The embassy connections, like the networks, existed prior to Operation Pedro Pan, for purposes such as providing sanctuary to adult Cubans in danger because of counterrevolutionary activities.[4]

Some people who obtained visa waivers reproduced and sold them. If the seller was part of the underground, he or she was shut out of further underground activities upon being discovered.[5] Although it is impossible to estimate the amount of trafficking that took place, it may have been significant, given the ease of doing it.

There were ways to obtain visa waivers other than through the schools, churches, and direct or indirect underground connections. A person could legitimately obtain a waiver signed by Father Walsh from the Swiss Embassy.[6] The United States conducted its minimal diplomatic business in Cuba through Switzerland's embassy in Havana after the break in diplomatic relations. Still, obtaining exit papers in such a manner was a bureaucratic and often fruitless endeavor. Besides, Cubans who wanted to leave Cuba or to send their children away generally wished to do so expeditiously. They feared that a slight change in the political atmosphere could shut down the avenues to emigration.

After the first few months of 1961, many people in Cuba fortunate enough to have a relative or friend in Miami could ask that person to request a visa waiver (either a visa waiver signed by Walsh for any child or, in the case of an adult, a regular waiver requested by a "first degree relative"). The relative could have then sent the visa waiver in the regular mail or with someone returning to Cuba. Yet, since the Cuban government did not respect the privacy of correspondence and because the frequency of returning to Cuba was minimal, these were not the preferred means of securing a visa waiver.

Besides sending the paperwork directly to Cuba, a relative working on behalf of someone on the island could take a visa waiver in that person's name to airline officials at Miami International Airport (MIA). There it was placed on file. KLM and Pan American Airlines employees in Miami regularly gave official notification to their colleagues in Havana of people whose visa waivers were on file at MIA. At that point, company officials in Cuba produced a standardized written document for each of those individuals stating that their visa waivers were awaiting them in Miami. For several months those forms from the airlines were acceptable exit documents for Cuban officials.[7]

At times airline employees in Havana, particularly those who worked for KLM, produced the standardized forms for Cubans who in reality had no documentation awaiting them in Miami. As Cuban officials could not distinguish between those who truly had documents in Miami and those who did not, they accepted the forms. The airline connection was open until the fall of 1961, when the Castro regime forced its citizens to go exclusively through Cuban bureaucratic channels when purchasing airline tickets. With that reform, the government demanded to see either the visa waiver or the person's name on the lists sent from Miami.[8]

Walsh attributed Operation Pedro Pan's success to keeping the amount of paperwork between Miami and Cuba minimal. He also credited Marxist inefficiency. According to him, "no one is taught to ask questions" in such a system. Obviously, if a person's papers seemed to be in order, officials were not trained to question their validity.[9]

Funding the exodus also posed an interesting challenge. By 1961 a person who sought to leave Cuba legally had to purchase a round-trip airline ticket with a $25.00 money order obtained in U.S. dollars. During the early months of Pedro Pan, when it was expected that only several hundred children would be smuggled out, the requirement was met by the process mentioned earlier, whereby U.S. businessmen in Miami channeled the money through the Catholic Welfare Bureau and carefully selected citizens in Miami to the W. Henry Smith Agency in Havana. Unfortunately, the funds were not nearly enough to finance the passage of the more than 14,000 children who came via Pedro Pan over the twenty-two months of its operation.

Some people in Cuba sent U.S. dollars directly to Father Walsh to use in purchasing money orders. Walsh readily complied. When dollars became more scarce in Cuba, Walsh recalled, people used creative means to send him the cash: "There were kids [who] had gone hunting under seat cushions and in the house, the drawers . . . and collected dimes and quarters and fifty-cent pieces, dollar bills and everything else. They attached them to pieces of cardboard . . . and scotch-taped them."[10] In addition to being sent by mail, the pieces of cardboard were sometimes smuggled in diplomatic pouches or by the spouses of Western diplomats who visited Miami.

In some instances, relatives or friends already in the United States purchased money orders for those seeking to leave Cuba. Walsh bought many others with donations he received to help Cuban refugees. He remembered sending $10,000 to $15,000 worth of money orders to Cuba with the instructions that they be used for those who were most in economic need.[11]

The federal government also assisted in financing Operation Pedro Pan. In July 1961 the U.S. government arranged to defray the cost of transporting Cubans who were issued visa waivers on or before July 21. Although the actual numbers are unclear, at least a few Pedro Pan children were likely beneficiaries.[12]

The work of those involved with Operation Pedro Pan inside Cuba was complex, uncertain, and risky. As mentioned earlier, it is impossible to know the number of people involved in the networks or any other facet of the operation. It was presumably several hundred, if not thousands. The stories of those who seemed most deeply involved in Pedro Pan, as well as some who participated for a short time at different points in the networks, deserve to be told.

Francisco ("Pancho") Finlay, the grandson of Carlos Finlay, the heralded Cuban physician who discovered the cause of yellow fever at the turn of the century, was connected to Ruston Academy through his wife, Berta de la Portilla de Finlay. She taught at the school. Both were part of the five-person committee that James Baker formed before leaving Cuba.

As KLM's general manager for Cuba and the Caribbean, Pancho Finlay played a decisive role in Operation Pedro Pan. It was he who secured spaces aboard KLM flights for children as well as adults seeking to leave Cuba.[13] In the mass hysteria of the early 1960s, planes of refugees were often overloaded, and on numerous occasions adults were asked to carry unaccompanied children on their laps. Sometimes the airlines were unable to take passengers' luggage because of the excess weight. It was not unusual for Cubans on those flights to have to wait several weeks for their luggage to arrive in Miami.[14]

It was Finlay who approved the false statements presented to Cuban officials stating that children (and presumably some adults) had visa waivers on file at MIA. Margarita Fuentes, an active member of Cuba's Catholic Youth who began working at KLM in Havana in May 1961, described collaborating with Finlay in the creation of the false statements:

> He [Finlay] was aware of everything that was going on. . . . I remember the cards used to come from here [Miami] saying that the visa was approved. So somebody in the office would just prepare the paperwork. This friend of ours who worked with the Catholic Youth Organization, who was from Bayamo, asked me one time about visas for the children. When I approached Finlay, he said, "Just write them up." So [from then on] he would just give me a list and then we would fill out [the statements] even if they [notifications of visa waivers in Miami] never arrived.[15]

Finlay and de la Portilla were likewise active in securing British visas on children's passports. Individuals on their networks collected the passports, and the couple passed them along to associates with embassy contacts.[16]

The danger of being caught with such passports was always present. James Baker remembered one of the couple's close calls:

> One day [Berta] said to her husband, "Pancho, I'm a little concerned about having all these passports here. I'm going to take them to the Dutch Embassy," and she went down to see the ambassador's wife and left those passports there. The next day they [the police] came and searched their house. They [Pancho and Berta] were in prison for two or three days. They [police] didn't find anything. But they said, "What are all these names of students?" She said, "Well, that was because Mr. Baker, who was the head of Ruston Academy, left the names for scholarships in the United States, and when he left I just took over the names."[17]

Clearly, the Finlays ran risks. Baker further revealed the possible extent of the Dutch government's role in Operation Pedro Pan. Such participation was not surprising—after all, Pancho Finlay was able to do all he did while working for the Netherlands' national airline.

The Finlays were also active in passing visa waivers to private school officials and underground organizations for wide-scale distribution, and

Pancho used his friendship with Pan American Airlines officials to help children leave Cuba. According to one estimate, the husband-and-wife team were responsible for aiding almost five thousand children find sanctuary in the United States.[18] Their own vast network included members of their families such as Berta's sister, Esther.[19] Finlay and de la Portilla died years later in exile in the United States.

Sergio Giquel and Serafina Lastra de Giquel were also close friends of the Bakers and, like the Finlays, part of James Baker's original committee. Sergio, an orthodontist, was involved with the operation from its inception by running messages between Miami and Havana during the few weeks Baker and Walsh were attempting to rescue children on U.S. student visas.[20] Serafina, the landscape artist who designed Ruston Academy's grounds, was active in distributing visa waivers and collecting passports to obtain British visas. She personally delivered documentation throughout Havana during the early days of the operation. Sergio died in Havana a few years after Pedro Pan's end. Serafina went to prison soon afterward for anti-Castro activities.[21]

Probably no person connected with Operation Pedro Pan was more deeply involved than Penny Powers, an Englishwoman and the fifth member of Baker's Ruston committee. As an English teacher at Ruston, she was well connected to American circles in Cuba and to the Cuban underground. A stout, strong-looking woman with short-cropped hair, Powers was the only person involved with the program who had any experience in child refugee movements. A nurse by training, she had been an important figure in helping Jewish children escape from Nazi-occupied Europe to her native Britain.[22]

After James Baker departed, many considered Powers to be Pedro Pan's principal figure inside Cuba. Because Powers never left Cuba, Pedro Pan operatives who were later exiled feared for her safety and kept her role a virtual secret for more than thirty years. In fact, Walsh spoke of her publicly for the first time during an interview for the dissertation that became this book. Yet others had preceded Walsh's acknowledgment, believing that the Cuban government would not punish a woman more than ninety years old for her activities thirty years earlier. Nevertheless, Powers's role remained to a great extent shrouded in mystery as late as the late 1990s.

Despite the general silence, some facts about Powers were clear. It was Powers who was the main contact with the British Embassy. She received authorization from her government to stamp British visas for travel to Jamaica.[23] She also enlisted the support of British diplomats. A certain British chargé d'affaires, according to Walsh, "pushed the limits of diplomatic immunity."[24] Before Cuba declared him a persona non grata, the British Foreign Office pulled him off the island.

In addition to her network activities, Powers herself distributed visa waivers and stamped passports directly—a big risk, since she provided documentation not only for Pedro Pan children but also for adults involved in the underground.[25]

Because she was a teacher at a private school, Powers had a number of contacts with other private schools in Cuba, and she played a key role in supplying visa waivers and British visas there when it became apparent that the schools were to be shut down. Powers also established a small, informal language school for the families of diplomats, where she secretly received documents from foreign embassies.[26] Powers was the only major figure involved with Operation Pedro Pan from its inception to its completion.

Powers's role and that of the British government were significant. The British not only permitted the use of their visas but also allowed their embassy and its personnel to be used for such clandestine activities. In fact, it was often British diplomats who transported money orders from Walsh to Pedro Pan participants in Cuba.[27]

Also active in Operation Pedro Pan were members of the family of Ramon Grau San Martin, one of Cuba's most popular democratic political figures prior to the Castro Revolution. Grau had served as Cuba's president for several weeks during the 1933 Revolution and again from 1944 to 1948. He maintained a large household in Havana, as well as a sizable political following. Among his entourage were his niece Leopoldina and nephew Ramon, nicknamed Polita and Mongo. Polita's political activism began with the struggle against the Machado dictatorship during the early 1930s. As a sixteen-year-old, she served as Cuba's first lady during her unmarried uncle's short stint as president after Machado's overthrow. Her younger brother Mongo was also active as his uncle's personal secretary and eventually as a representative in Cuba's legislature.

When Batista orchestrated his coup d'etat in 1952 and established his dictatorship, Polita Grau joined the resistance to him. As part of the anti-Batista movement, Polita left Cuba to join Antonio Varona, an exiled politician and associate of her uncle, in Miami. Suspicious of the motives of Batista's successor, she remained in Miami for five months after the dictator's overthrow. Horrified by Castro's turn toward Communism, Polita Grau once again found herself part of an underground movement to overthrow the Cuban government.[28]

Polita joined a counterrevolutionary group led by Varona, Movimiento de Rescate Revolucionario (Revolutionary Rescue Movement). The actions of the group ranged from finding sanctuary for underground operatives to attempting assassination of Fidel Castro. Polita, as women's coordinator, established a spy ring that reached every corner of Cuba. Her social position as Grau San Martin's niece gave her some flexibility, as the ensuing public relations embarrassment had her uncle gone into exile would have been great for the Castro regime at the time.[29]

Polita Grau first became aware of Pedro Pan when a group of women, allegedly sent by Penny Powers, approached her brother in the spring of 1961 and asked for his help in distributing documents to children. Polita offered her brother the services of three trustworthy women in her network: Alicia Thomas, Beatriz Perez Lopez, and Hilda Feo.[30] Her brother's role was significant, and Polita herself was active in distributing exit papers and airline tickets. Using her Rescate network, she received and fulfilled the requests of many families. Because she was well known, former politicians from the provinces who had been associated with her uncle's political party asked her personally for documents. She received the same requests from priests and nuns she knew, seeking to help children in their schools and congregations. Polita later said the Cuban Baptist Church in particular had secured a number of visa waivers from her.[31]

Polita also worked closely with Israel Padilla, a Rescate member who had produced a phony U.S. visa stamp. She recalled how they used Padilla's stamp and the assistance they received from the Panamanian Embassy:

> We had a quota of three hundred per week.... We would get together once a week at the Panamanian Embassy, where at the moment Elvira Jované de Zayas was in charge of Panamanian businesses. She offered us her house so that we could fix the passports in peace without thinking, There are the police, they are going to catch us. There were three of us: Padilla, Toribio Bravo, and me. We filled out the passports . . . they came out perfectly. She would not let us take the passports into the street. She took them out in her car so that we

would have no problems. Then from my house we distributed the passports. Padilla took his, I took mine.[32]

The Padilla visas were used for both children and adults. The brilliance of the phony visa was that it was American and could not be checked for authenticity since the U.S. Embassy was closed. The visas were accepted by both Cuban and U.S. authorities.

Polita remembered times when it was difficult finding spaces aboard airplanes for children. In those cases she utilized the services of her good friend Juanita Castro, Fidel Castro's sister, who was active in the struggle against her brother and who had connections at Havana's airport.[33]

Ramon ("Mongo") Grau, like others involved in Operation Pedro Pan, was zealous in anti-Castro activities, including assassination attempts against the dictator. Like his sister Polita, he was more untouchable than others in the underground because of his uncle's prestige.

Using Grau San Martin's Havana home as a base and assisted by the three women from his sister's group, Mongo parceled out visa waivers, Padilla visas, money orders, and airline tickets to those in his network for island-wide distribution. His uncle's house, as the home of an ex-president, had many visitors daily. Thus underground operatives could call at the house without arousing the suspicion of the G.2 headquarters across the street.[34]

The timing of Polita and Mongo's involvement was critical for Operation Pedro Pan's future success. After the Bay of Pigs invasion of April 1961, many underground networks collapsed, and numerous operatives were either rounded up by the government or forced to flee the island. The Graus and their associates filled much of the underground vacuum and were largely responsible for keeping Operation Pedro Pan alive.

Polita and Mongo were both arrested in 1965, three years after the conclusion of Operation Pedro Pan, for political activities unassociated with the children's exodus. By then, neither their family name nor the government's desire to keep their uncle in Cuba could protect them. Polita remained in a political prison until 1979. Mongo was released in 1986. Grau San Martin died in 1969, having seen his nephew and niece for the last time as Fidel Castro's prisoners.

Like Polita Grau, Sara del Toro Odio had been politically active since the anti-Machado struggle of the early 1930s and was deeply involved in the struggle against Batista during the 1950s. Along with her husband

Amador Odio, who owned Trafico y Transporte, S.A., one of Cuba's largest trucking companies, she was a strong supporter of Castro in early 1959. When the leader shifted to Communism, however, del Toro and her husband joined Movimiento Revolucionario del Pueblo (People's Revolutionary Movement), a group of disaffected former Castro supporters.

Del Toro's anti-Castro activities were such that she feared for the lives of the older of her ten children. When she brought them to the safety of the United States in January 1961, del Toro made the acquaintance of Father Walsh through her good friend Maurice Ferre—a young, wealthy Puerto Rican who later became mayor of Miami.[35] Ferre had earlier donated a house near downtown Miami for Walsh to use as a home for Cuban boys. Upon Ferre's recommendation, Walsh asked del Toro if she would take visa waivers back to Cuba for distribution. She agreed and left for Havana with a suitcase filled with visa waivers.[36]

Although Sara del Toro knew that Penny Powers and others in Cuba were working on Pedro Pan, she had no connection with any of them. She distributed visa waivers, primarily from her home, to whoever needed them, whether or not they were known to her. Del Toro said later, "I gave more to people I did not know. We would get together at my farm and I gave it to them there or likewise at the FOCSA . . . different places. Many were in the underground who were desperate to get their children out because they were afraid."[37]

Like others who worked on Pedro Pan, del Toro helped many adults escape Cuba. She was active in the underground and Pedro Pan until she and her husband were arrested in the fall of 1961. They both served several years in Castro's political prisons.

There were many who worked under Pedro Pan's principal figures, and their contributions were diverse and significant. One was Elena de la Torriente, from a prominent Havana family deeply involved in the underground. Among other activities, de la Torriente was connected to the Baker committee's network during the months prior to the Bay of Pigs invasion, through her acquaintance with Margarita Oteiza, a Ruston teacher and a primary contact with Baker's committee. De la Torriente was active mainly in assisting underground members' children leave Cuba. When a member asked her for help, she contacted Oteiza (or, after the latter left Cuba, another in the Baker committee network), who then secured exit papers from the Baker committee. Before the closing of the U.S. Embassy, de la

Torriente also used her own contacts there to help both children and adults leave Cuba.[38]

Albertina O'Farrill was another shining light in Operation Pedro Pan. The ex-wife of Cuba's one-time ambassador to Portugal and the Netherlands, O'Farrill was one of Pedro Pan's chief embassy contacts, working closely with both the Baker committee and the Graus. Through her connections, O'Farrill received visa waivers and money orders from foreign diplomats and delivered the paperwork to the appropriate operatives. It was also O'Farrill who facilitated Penny Powers's establishment of her small language school. She likewise helped hundreds, perhaps thousands, of endangered Cuban adults escape the island through embassies. O'Farrill served fourteen years in Castro's political prisons for her antigovernment activities.[39]

The many people working on Operation Pedro Pan in Cuba reflected the diversity of the Cuban underground. Nevertheless, there were some consistencies among those at the program's highest levels. Most of them were dedicated to conspiring against Castro and their overall activities outweighed their participation in Operation Pedro Pan. Most also helped endangered adults escape the island. Politically active before Castro's assumption of power, many had participated in Batista's overthrow.

Those heading the exodus from Cuba came almost exclusively from the island's former elite—a crucial characteristic since it is the social, economic, intellectual, and political leadership in most societies who are well-connected to the outside world. Working on the residuals of their former positions, these Cubans were able to help children of all social classes find freedom in the United States. They all possessed a fierce belief in democracy that predated their opposition to Castro and Batista. For the most part, they were associated with Cuba's democratic, liberal political tradition. Sadly, however, they paid a price for their courage and devotion; although none was reportedly convicted of any crimes directly associated with Operation Pedro Pan, many served long sentences in a brutal political system for other pro-democratic activities in Cuba and lived out their years in exile.

Five

Helping Cubans Escape Tyranny:
The Washington Details

The right of people to freedom of thought and religious belief has reverberated throughout our society from the days when the early settlers came to our shores to escape a tyranny that was intolerable. The refugees now coming to the United States from Cuba are, in many respects, following this tradition.
Katherine Brownell Oettinger, chief of the HEW Children's Bureau, 1962

John F. Kennedy's assumption of the U.S. presidency in January 1961 led to both favorable and unfavorable developments for Cuban exiles. First of all, alterations in the military strategy aimed at ousting Fidel Castro were unfortunate for Cuban exiles: Kennedy's policy, instead of overthrowing Castro, inadvertently allowed the dictator to consolidate his rule in Cuba. Cuban refugees in the United States fared better when the Kennedy administration inherited the problem of dealing with them, as the administration established the largest, most comprehensive refugee program in U.S. history.

President Kennedy's first move was to delegate responsibility for Cuban refugees to the Department of Health, Education, and Welfare (HEW), headed by Secretary Abraham Ribicoff. President Eisenhower's practice had been to deal with refugee matters through special administration representatives such as Tracy Voorhees.

In a January 27, 1961, directive, President Kennedy charged Ribicoff with "directing the Cuban Refugee activities now being conducted by the Executive branch of the Federal Government and to make an on-the-scene investigation of the problem within the next week."[1] Secretary Ribicoff, who conducted his investigation in Miami before the end of January, within days presented to Kennedy a report that reemphasized the need for a comprehensive aid program. The president outlined specific goals for assisting Cuban refugees on February 3, 1961:[2]

(1) Providing all possible *assistance to voluntary relief agencies* in providing daily necessities for needy refugees, for resettling as many refugees as possible, and for securing jobs for them.

(2) Obtaining the assistance of both private and governmental agencies to provide useful *employment opportunities* for displaced Cubans, consistent with the over all employment situation in Florida.

(3) Providing funds for the *resettlement* of refugees to other areas.

(4) Furnishing *financial assistance* to meet basic maintenance requirements of needy Cuban refugees in the Miami area and as required in communities of resettlement.

(5) Providing for essential *health services* for refugees.

(6) Furnishing Federal assistance for local public *school operating costs* in the Miami area.

(7) Initiating measures to augment *training and educational opportunities* for Cuban refugees.

(8) Providing financial aid for the care and protection of *unaccompanied children*—the most defenseless and troubled group among the refugee population.

(9) Undertaking surplus food distribution.

Kennedy stated, "I hope that these measures will be understood as an immediate expression of the firm desire of the people of the United States to be of tangible assistance to the refugees until such time as better circumstances enable them to return to their permanent homes in health, in confidence, and with unimpaired pride."[3] The Cuban Refugee Program was designed to carry out the president's objectives.

The financing and administration of aid to Cuban refugees went through a series of modifications. President Eisenhower's assistance plan of early January 1961 had received a $1 million allocation from the President's Contingency Fund under the Mutual Security Act of 1954. Kennedy's extension to the end of the fiscal year (June 30, 1961) drew $4 million from the same source. During fiscal year 1962, funding from the contingency fund was authorized by the Foreign Assistance Act of 1961, as amended. On June 28, 1962, the Migration and Refugee Assistance Act was passed, and from then on, Congress appropriated funds for the Cuban Refugee Program.[4] In its first few years, the program received: fiscal 1961, $4,089,000; fiscal 1962, $38,557,000; fiscal 1963, $56,310,000.

Initially, HEW assigned the Cuban Refugee Program's administration to the department's commissioner of social security; in January 1963 the program was transferred to HEW's newly organized Welfare Administration and in August 1967 to the newly formed Social and Rehabilitation Service within HEW.[5] The Cuban Refugee Program's administrators used the services of both governmental and nongovernmental agencies. Within HEW itself, the Bureau of Family Assistance oversaw financial assistance to needy refugees, and the Children's Bureau administered the Cuban Children's Program at the federal level. HEW's Public Health Service oversaw medical and dental services, and its Office of Education supervised overall child education, language and vocational courses for adults, and education loans for college-age refugees. The U.S. Department of Labor's Employment Service worked closely with HEW in studying the refugees' educational background and then helping to find employment, in cooperation with state agencies.

The Florida State Department of Public Welfare became responsible for distributing federal financial assistance and surplus food, in most cases through private agencies that were subcontracted. Public Welfare also acted as the intermediary between HEW and the agencies involved in the Cuban Children's Program (discussed in greater detail later).

Local South Florida public and private agencies, including the Dade County Public Schools and the Dade County Health Department, took part in administering the federal program. The University of Miami offered refresher courses for refugees with certain professional training.[6]

HEW used four national voluntary agencies to help settle Cuban Refugees outside the Miami impact area: the Catholic Relief Services of the National Catholic Welfare Conference; the Church World Service of the National Council of Churches; the International Rescue Committee; and the United Hebrew Immigrant Aid Society (United HIAS).[7] Miami officials, although sympathetic to the refugees' plight, were mostly concerned with their relocation, as the city had by far the highest concentration of Cuban refugees in the United States. In fact, Miami ultimately became home to more Cubans than any city in the world with the exception of Havana.

Nationwide, an array of community groups participated in the Cuban Refugee Program, especially in receiving those who resettled. The out-of-town entities included state and local welfare departments, public and private children's agencies, local churches and civic groups, and institutions of higher learning. The fusion of public and private agencies was the essence of the program. The federal government used existing agencies partly because there was no time to set up separate entities and partly because the Cuban refugee crisis was seen as temporary.[8]

The Cuban Refugee Program acted as the nerve center for relief activities. It set up its first operational base, the Cuban Refugee Emergency Center, on N.W. 3rd Avenue in the former offices of the Dade County Board of Public Instruction.[9] The headquarters was soon moved to 600 Biscayne Boulevard in Miami, a building known as the Miami News Tower when it had housed the offices of the *Miami Daily News*, previous to 1957. Known as the Freedom Tower to most Cuban Americans, the Mediterranean-style structure was later viewed nostalgically as Miami's own Ellis Island. In 1997 Cuban American businessman and political leader Jorge Mas Canosa purchased the by-then abandoned and dilapidated building and pledged to restore it "to its original architectural luster."[10] Mas Canosa, who died shortly thereafter, planned to create a Cuban refugee museum. That burden now rests on his descendants.

Although Cuban exiles were not required to register with or use the services of the Cuban Refugee Center, the vast majority did so. From the center, program officials treated refugees and their families on a case-by-case basis to determine such facts as job skills and family composition, toward the goal of resettlement. The refugees were also given medical examinations and inoculations. The Red Cross provided English-Spanish dictionaries and survival kits that included basic toiletries.[11] Financial assistance, clothes, and surplus food were also distributed from the center.

The freedom of Cuban refugees was truly remarkable. Although encouraged to resettle, they were not forced to leave Miami. In traditional programs, particularly in post–World War II Europe, camps usually held refugees indefinitely. The Cuban Refugee Program, on the other hand, did not restrict the movement of Cuban exiles. John Thomas, the program's director, believed that the reason was the "traditional dislike of Americans for camp set-ups" and the experience with such camps in the Hungarian program. Moreover, Thomas pointed out, Cuban refugees were viewed as temporary exiles.[12]

Consideration as a Cuban refugee eligible for the program required that (1) a person was a national of Cuba living in the Miami area or in another area as a result of resettlement under the program; (2) the person had left Cuba on or after January 1, 1959, or the director of the center found that withholding benefits would tend to defeat the purposes of the program; and (3) the person bore identification from the U.S. Immigration and Naturalization Service and was (a) a parolee under section 212(d)(5) of the Immigration and Naturalization Act, or (b) an alien granted indefinite voluntary departure, or (c) an alien who was a permanent resident of the United States. Any person could be denied assistance if the center's director believed that it would be "inimical to the interests of the United States."[13]

Although the United States provided sanctuary and temporary assistance for thousands of refugees after World War II, the Cuban Refugee Program was the first of its kind. In other programs, the refugees were processed in other nations and thereafter brought to the United States in an orderly, planned fashion. During the Cuban influx, the United States became, for the first time in its history, a country of first asylum for refugees.[14] The U.S. government had no way of knowing how many refugees would arrive in any given month, week, or day. Public and private agencies met that challenge as efficiently and professionally as was realistic.

In keeping with point number eight of Kennedy's directive to HEW Secretary Ribicoff, the Cuban Refugee Program provided "financial aid for the care and protection of unaccompanied children—the most defenseless and troubled group among the refugee population." When Ribicoff visited Miami in late January 1961, he was aware of the problem of unaccompanied children and of Father Walsh's work on their behalf, and the secretary sought to speak to the young priest at a public meeting during his visit. Because of Walsh's concern about keeping the Pedro Pan aspect of the children's program secret, he instead met with Ribicoff privately.

Ribicoff told Walsh that he had spoken to the Children's Bureau about working with the Catholic Welfare Bureau and other local volunteer agencies on the details of a purchase-of-care contract.[15] Although Walsh had been promised federal money from Eisenhower's allocation for Cuban refugees, the purchase-of-care contracts would formally bind him to the soon-to-be-established Cuban Refugee Program. That was good news, since the federal government would thus become committed to the goal of helping Cuban children, and funding would be permanent. Negotiations between the federal government, Florida's state government, and the private agencies providing care began in February.

The federal government, through HEW's Children's Bureau, concluded a contract with the Florida State Department of Public Welfare in late February 1961. The state Department of Public Welfare agreed to act as the agent for HEW in the distribution of federal funds for the care of unaccompanied children. Florida's Department of Public Welfare, in turn, subcontracted the local private voluntary child care organizations that had already been working with unaccompanied Cuban children: Walsh's Catholic Welfare Bureau of the Diocese of Miami; the Children's Service Bureau (Protestant, nondenominational); the Jewish Family and Children's Service of the Greater Miami Jewish Federation; and United HIAS. The contracts were signed on March 1, 1961.[16]

The private organizations provided the actual care. Because the problem of unaccompanied Cuban children was considered temporary, custody remained with parents in Cuba.[17] Walsh's desires in November had thus been secured: The children's religious heritage was guarded, and licensed organizations provided child care, subsidized by public money.

The process of meeting the children at the point of entry, Miami International Airport (MIA), remained relatively unchanged. When the children arrived in Miami, agents of the Catholic Welfare Bureau and United HIAS were on the premises to carry out their overall responsibilities, but it was usually Walsh's organization that actually awaited the children. If there was a Protestant or Jewish unaccompanied child among the refugees, the Catholic Welfare Bureau contacted the corresponding private agency.[18]

The private Miami agencies attempted to provide foster or group care in the area, but because of the sheer numbers of children, they were forced to call on the services of nationwide welfare organizations among their religious affiliates. The most elaborate network was created by the Catholic Welfare Bureau, as the overwhelming majority of the children were at least nominally Catholic. The Miami agencies handled all direct transactions with the out-of-town agencies that provided assistance.

In compliance with Father Walsh's desires of November 1960, the Cuban children were cared for by competent child-care agencies licensed by the state in which they operated. Florida's Department of Public Welfare checked with other state welfare departments on the agencies' qualifications. Because the federal government had assumed responsibility for the Cuban children's care and protection, "the usual guarantees against public dependency covered in state regulations regarding the importation of children were not necessary."[19]

For administrative and eligibility reasons, the Children's Bureau defined an unaccompanied Cuban refugee as "a child in the Miami impact area at the time service is initiated, whose parent or relative cannot provide care and supervision for him, who is in need of foster care, and who meets the definition of a refugee as defined by the federal government."[20]

The federal government ultimately called the program the "Unaccompanied Cuban Refugee Children's Program." The local agencies, however, continued calling it the Cuban Children's Program, the name used in this book.

The federal government funded the Cuban Children's Program through per diem payments on a reimbursement basis. In determining the amount paid, HEW considered the costs of a child's board and care, clothing, medical care, school supplies, incidentals, casework services, and administrative expenses. Other considerations were the diversity in living costs across the United States, adolescents' greater consumption of food and clothing, and the winter clothing needed in the country's colder regions. In the end, HEW decided to reimburse each participating agency $6.50 per day per child for group care and $5.50 for foster care. Of that amount, the Miami agency retained fifty cents for administrative costs. The federal government also reimbursed transportation of children to out-of-town placements.[21] All private agencies received supplemental funds from their religious organizations.[22]

The Cuban Children's Program had probably the greatest long-range impact on child welfare procedures in the area of financial organization. The startup of the program brought to light the outdated nature of methods of cost analysis, and the Children's Bureau estimates were sometimes inaccurate or incomplete. The Children's Bureau then began conducting regional workshops to introduce new cost analysis procedures, based on Martin Wolins's work *A Manual for Cost Analysis in Institutions for Children* (Child Welfare League of America, 1962). Local welfare agencies across the country thus not only gained experience in placements and child care but were also able to update their cost analysis procedures.

The Cuban Children's Program brought other lessons as well. It highlighted interracial foster home placements, as some Cuban children of Chinese and African heritage were placed in white homes. The system of small group homes used initially in Miami for teenage Cuban boys found application elsewhere.[23] Not to be discounted was the program's successful experience in cooperative efforts among local, state, federal, and private institutions.

Among the precedents it established, the Cuban Children's Program was the first time the federal government aided refugee children by funding voluntary private agencies.[24] In fact, when federal money was first promised, Father Walsh had a difficult time convincing his superiors in the Diocese of Miami that it would actually be paid. When the first reimbursement check came through in February 1961, Walsh said later, the diocese, through his actions, "was $75,000 in debt, which was a lot of money in those days. The first check we got was for $75,000. The diocese was breathing down my back and telling me that I was headed for absolute destruction because 'if you think you're going to get money out of the federal government, you're crazy. Church agencies don't get money.' When that first check arrived, I sent it to the chancellor, and I sent him a photocopy with the words 'He who laughs last laughs best.' I don't think they ever forgave me for that."[25] According to Walsh, later legislation influenced by his work included Senator Barry Goldwater's amendment to the Economic Opportunity Act, which gave religious agencies the right to receive funds provided for in the legislation. The amendment's justification was the Cuban Children's Program.

Many Cuban children, especially Roman Catholics, were sent to private religious schools. During an audit in Tallahassee, HEW raised the issue of using federal money to pay tuition at Catholic schools. Frank Kraft, director of the Florida State Department of Public Welfare, took the matter to Father Walsh, who responded in writing to HEW. Walsh's statement pointed out that the money was used not as aid to private schools but as assistance to Cuban children, and that those who were in loco parentis had the constitutional right to decide how their children were educated. The statement was signed by Kraft and Ribicoff, and the question was not raised again. Cuban children continued attending private religious schools until the Cuban Children's Program ended in 1981.[26]

Six

The Cuban Children's Program:
Umbrella Group Cares for the
Wards of Pedro Pan

Anyone who welcomes a little child such as this in my name,
welcomes me, and anyone who welcomes me, welcomes not me
but the one who sent me.
Mark 9:37

Operation Pedro Pan owed its existence to the Cuban Children's Program. Without the means to care for Cuban children, the idea of rescuing them from Communism by bringing them to the United States would have been preposterous. About half of the youngsters rescued by Operation Pedro Pan required the care that the Cuban Children's Program devised.

In spite of the connection between the two rescue efforts, they were distinct entities. In fact, the care-giving program continued to accept Cuban refugee children well after the exodus through Pedro Pan ended. Although the number of participants in the Cuban Children's Program shrank dramatically after the program's Pedro Pan children were discharged, it continued on a comparatively modest level until 1981.

The beneficiaries of the Cuban Children's Program until 1962 were considered students to a degree, being of school age and sent to the United States by parents who wanted to shelter them from the Communist government's monopolization of Cuban education. The perception of the children as student refugees was the basis of the term used to describe their placements in permanent care: *beca*, which translates into English as scholarship. Despite their student status, however, the children were in the United States primarily to be protected from Communism. Their parents' dual opportunity to rescue their children from Cuba and to secure their education was the creation of Father Walsh's organization and the other agencies that cooperated with the Cuban Children's Program.

The Jewish Community

The American Jewish community was in the forefront of aiding Cuban refugees, both children and adults. Its welfare organizations had a permanent presence at the Cuban Refugee Center, and its representatives met the arrival of daily flights from Havana. The community played a role in virtually all features of the Cuban Refugee Program, although its main focus was to help Cuban Jews in their time of great need.

Finding help for Cuban Jews was no small task, as more than two-thirds of the island's 10,000 Jews had gone into U.S. exile by October 1962.[1] Many were cared for by the local Jewish Family and Children's Service, an agency of the Greater Miami Jewish Federation. They had the help of United HIAS, the "national migration agency of the Jewish Community in America."[2] It was ironic, if not tragic, that international Jewish migration agencies had placed European Jews in Cuba a generation earlier to escape persecution after World War I. United HIAS's executive director, James P. Rice, stated to the U.S. Senate Judiciary Committee in 1962, "It is a special tragedy . . . today to see refugees who came to Cuba a generation ago as babes in arms now coming out themselves as refugees once again with their babies and their children."[3]

United HIAS, a strong national organization, had powerful resources to assist the local and comparatively small Jewish Family and Children's Service. Such aid included permanent port and dock workers as well as trained resettlement and welfare personnel.[4] Financial aid was also made available, particularly during the period before federal money was allocated to help refugees during the final weeks of the Eisenhower administration.

As signatories to the purchase-of-care contracts, the Jewish Family and Children's Service found foster care for children in Miami, and United HIAS took on the main burden of placing children outside the Miami area. In all, the two agencies placed 145 children in Jewish foster homes, 117 of them outside the Miami area.[5]

Like children placed by the other agencies, the Jewish children often developed intimate ties to their foster families. The combination of a family's compassion with the Cuban youngsters' gratitude and emotional need cemented many of those relationships. In the early 1990s, Evelyn and Ben Clein wrote a letter to the editor of the *Miami Herald* that testified to such bonds:

> When some families from Temple Beth Am were asked if they would take a Jewish child being smuggled out of Cuba, we were happy to volunteer. A few weeks later at 7 a.m., there was a knock at the door, and a man stood there with a beautiful 7-year-old boy who could not speak a word of English. We could not speak a word of Spanish. All I could do was take him in my arms and cry with him as he kept calling for his mother. We contacted her in Havana that afternoon and spoke with her through an interpreter. In about a week and with the help of our daughter, Judi, who was about 12, he felt comfortable with us. We loved him. We got a call from Jewish Family Service personnel, who told us that the boy had to be sent up North so that there would be room for other children in Miami. I told them that I would not give him up to resettle with more strangers, that he was just a baby. I called his uncle here and begged him to take the child, and he did. His uncle is now president of a major Miami bank. We were told to forget the boy and never try to find out where he is. However, we can't forget someone who was part of our heart. Wherever you are, Roberto, we think of you often. God bless you.[6]

Protestant Placements

It was the responsibility of the Children's Service Bureau to provide care for all Protestant Cuban refugee children who were unaccompanied. Although the bureau took responsibility for nearly double the number of children overseen by the Jewish agencies, it had no permanent representative at MIA since its role was limited to assisting the few unaccompanied Protestant youngsters—not Cuban Protestants as a whole. When a Protestant child arrived, the Catholic Welfare Bureau usually took charge of the youngster until the Children's Service Bureau could be contacted.[7]

Initially the Children's Service Bureau encountered many difficulties. Unlike the Catholic and Jewish communities in the United States, the bureau had no network of licensed foster homes or group care facilities on which to call. Although there were many offers, few came from state-licensed providers. The wide array of Protestant denominations posed yet another challenge to placements, as the children and their parents insisted that denominational lines not be crossed.[8]

The Children's Service Bureau in the end placed no fewer than 267 children in foster care, at least 190 of them outside Miami. The saving grace was the Child Welfare League of America, which held a conference in the spring of 1962 to discuss the issue. As a result of that meeting, denominationally sponsored and nonsectarian child care agencies volunteered their services.[9]

State Agencies' Care of Children

The Florida State Department of Public Welfare, although chiefly concerned with administration, also carried a caseload of about ninety children. Most of their charges, who lived with foster families and in group care homes, had been sent by parents to relatives or friends in the United States, who later felt that they could no longer provide a good home.[10]

For the small number of disabled children, the Florida State Crippled Children's Commission generally stepped in, funded by the Children's Bureau.

The Role of Catholic Welfare

It was the Catholic Welfare Bureau that took on the brunt of the work in the Cuban Children's Program, since most of the refugee children were officially Catholic. The primary role it played had several aspects. After the Bay of Pigs, Operation Pedro Pan's few hundred child refugees became a wave of several thousand, and by 1962 the Catholic Welfare Bureau had created three transit centers on Miami's outskirts to receive unaccompanied Cuban children. The centers took in those who were not met at the airport by relatives or friends. If Jewish, the children were taken from the airport by United HIAS.

If a child who arrived at the transit center was Protestant, the Catholic Welfare Bureau contacted the Children's Service Bureau, which assumed responsibility as quickly as possible.[11] Some children were placed with relatives or friends in Miami a few days after arrival. The centers' main purpose was to shelter children temporarily until they could be placed in permanent care elsewhere. The intent was to make room for those who would arrive in the future; at no time did Walsh know how many children would arrive in a given day, week, or month, and no one could predict when the aerial migration would end. In other words, Operation Pedro Pan had a direct impact on the Cuban Children's Program, and geopolitics influenced the entire enterprise.

The Catholic Welfare Bureau worked closely with the National Conference of Catholic Charities and Catholic dioceses throughout the United States to find permanent places for the children. When children received word of their long-awaited placements, or becas, they usually reached their destinations within days. Although not always successful, the Catholic Welfare Bureau made every effort to keep brothers and sisters together when they left. For many children, the transit center experience was one of patiently waiting to learn their destination. Fortunately, many children were reunited with their parents before they left the centers.

At the centers the children lived in a Cuban atmosphere—the result of both deliberate efforts by the Catholic Welfare Bureau and the nature of the staff and fellow residents. Believing the children needed to feel as much at home as possible, the supervisors staged celebrations of Cuban holidays, dance parties for the teenagers with both Cuban and American music, and talent shows that included tributes to Cuban culture. There was a general reluctance by the staff to force assimilation.[12]

The children's spiritual needs were likewise met, through regular attendance at mass, the celebration of religious holidays, and group rosaries with the adults. For a time, a statuette of the Virgen de la Caridad—the Virgin of Charity, Cuba's patron—made its rounds of the camps.[13] The small statue had been smuggled from Cuba by anti-Castro operatives with the cooperation of foreign embassies. In later years a small shrine overlooking Biscayne Bay, La Ermita de la Caridad, was built in Coconut Grove to house the image.

In as many instances as possible, adult Cubans staffed the transit centers. Administration of the centers, for instance, was the work of exiled clerics from Cuba under the auspices of Father Walsh. The priests, brothers, and nuns had managed schools in Cuba and were familiar with a number of the children. Clerics from Cuba continued to provide supervision when the centers for older boys were merged and moved to another facility. The two other transit centers, which then housed girls and younger boys, were staffed by Cuban houseparents in addition to clerics. Beyond that, adult

Cuban exiles filled positions such as teachers, nurses, counselors, domestic workers, office workers, and various others. In 1992 Walsh said that Cuban exiles had made up about 95 percent of the staff at both the transit centers and other branches of the Catholic Welfare Bureau's local efforts on behalf of the Cuban Children's Program.[14]

In Walsh's view, the Cuban adults who worked for the Cuban Children's Program had suffered as much trauma as the children, enduring the general difficulties of life in exile and family separation, as well as having seen lifetime accomplishments stripped away. Among the Cuban adult workers in Miami were a former postmaster general and a former minister of education.[15] Most adult Cuban workers were college-educated.[16]

In many cases the Cuban adults and children developed quite close relationships, both being in awkward positions and feeling alone in a strange land. It was common for a child to grow so close to one of the adults that a surrogate parent-child relationship developed, as evidenced by the many cards and letters sent back by the children when they were placed outside Miami.

How the Children's Quarters Evolved

The background of the Catholic Welfare Bureau's first transit facility, the Kendall center, was tied to Dade County's integration of its child welfare facilities shortly before the onset of Operation Pedro Pan and the Cuban Children's Program. The facility in the Kendall area that the county vacated had been used to house dependent and delinquent African American children.[17] The Dade County Welfare Department offered the facility to Father Walsh. Years later he said that the county's generosity may have had something to do with its own fear of having to deal with unaccompanied Cuban children.[18] At any rate, the Catholic Welfare Bureau formally requested the use of the Kendall facility shortly after Christmas 1960.

Overcrowding at Kendall over the next several months led to the creation of two other transit centers in Dade County—one for older teenage boys and the other for girls and the youngest boys. Shortly afterward, Kendall was used exclusively to house boys between the ages of twelve and fourteen.[19]

In January 1961 Fernando Pruna and his wife became the first houseparents assigned to the Kendall facility. In late January Walsh asked Mother Thomas, who had administered an Ursuline Academy in Havana and had by then returned to the United States, to administer the Kendall operation. After some resistance because of her order's pre–Vatican II rules against working with boys, the mother superior finally relented. She was persuaded by Walsh, the bishop, and Archbishop Vagnozzi, an apostolic delegate visiting Miami.[20]

The nun's tenure at Kendall was brief, as Cuban Marist Brothers took over the operation in June 1961. The Marist Brothers were credited with providing structure and organized activities to the camp's frequently idle and bored child population.[21]

The Kendall complex consisted of three structures: a girls' cottage (when it housed girls), a double-wing boys' cottage with a kitchen and dining area, and a four-classroom building. Fortunately, the complex had large areas for recreation all around. Yet Kendall's lack of trees made it somewhat unattractive. Because it was used only as a temporary shelter for children en route to a more permanent destination, little effort was made to improve Kendall's appearance.[22]

At the height of Operation Pedro Pan, Kendall, like the other centers, buzzed with activity and was frequently plagued by overcrowding. According to an observer in 1962, "The camp was jammed to overcapacity, army surplus beds, three high, filled each building until there was barely enough room to pass through."[23] Since the center was used for transitory purposes only, however, there was little point in creating a sense of permanence.

When Dade County requested the return of its Kendall facility in 1962, Walsh arranged to move the children staying there to an unused U.S. Marine barracks at Opa-Locka airport. After a postponement caused by the Cuban missile crisis, the children moved in early 1963.[24] Jesuits from Cuba, who were running a permanent boys' home and had opened a school in Miami, were placed in charge in Opa-Locka when their home for boys was closed, and its residents also moved to the barracks.[25]

Camp Matecumbe was named for the Florida natives converted to Christianity by eighteenth-century Cuban missionaries. It became the Catholic Welfare Bureau's transit center for boys between the ages of fifteen and eighteen in mid-1961. A diocesan summer youth camp before the refugee crisis, Matecumbe held over three hundred boys during peak periods of Operation Pedro Pan and the Cuban Children's Program.[26]

Matecumbe was made a Catholic Welfare Bureau transit center when Pedro Pan grew to massive proportions. Although it was meant to be a temporary shelter, it held children for longer periods than Kendall because older teenage boys were the most difficult to place in foster family or group care.[27] Thus, Matecumbe took on more of a sense of permanence. Shortly after Matecumbe was made a transit center, Walsh handed the camp's administration to a Cuban Escolapio priest, Francisco Pala. He was assisted by a large staff of Cuban and American laity that included maintenance personnel, counselors, athletic coaches, teachers, nurses, and office workers.[28] Pala left Matecumbe in 1964, months before the facility's closing, when he was called away to a school in Fort Lauderdale run by his religious order. He was replaced by Christian Brothers from Cuba.[29]

Activities for the boys at Matecumbe were varied and structured. The camp included an olympic-sized swimming pool, sports programs headed by coaches, and nature walks, as well as classes. At the camp canteen, the boys could use their weekly allowances to buy sundries, candy and soda, and postage stamps for cards and letters to their estranged loved ones. Children at Matecumbe and elsewhere often saved their allowances to buy money orders for their parents to use in buying airline tickets in Cuba. Some used the money for their weekend excursions into downtown Miami.[30]

There was an air of permissiveness at Matecumbe. The boys, outside of meals and sleeping, were essentially free to roam the grounds and take part in numerous activities offered by the staff. The chaotic days of 1961 and 1962 caused chronic overcrowding. Bunks, stacked to the ceiling, were jammed into dormitory areas. Sometimes boys had to use the outdoor showers meant for bathers in the camp's swimming pool.[31] In spite of their discomfort the Matecumbe boys, like the children at other facilities, were all fed and cared for properly.

By 1963 conditions at Camp Matecumbe had improved dramatically, after the end of Operation Pedro Pan and of the pressure to relocate children. To create a greater sense of permanence, the Catholic Welfare Bureau constructed an all-purpose building, with large portions sectioned off into more spacious and private dormitories. The original cabins were returned to Matecumbe's regular summer visitors. The Cuban boys began attending local high schools, and Matecumbe received a permanent social work unit. The camp's library grew and hobbies, sports, field trips, and other recreational activities kept morale at the camp high.[32]

At one point the camp opened the experimental Matecumbe High

1. James Baker, the Cuban connection for children who fled Castro to Miami, was headmaster of Havana's Ruston Academy.

2. Cuban children in transit center pray before image of La Virgen de la Caridad. By permission of Operation Pedro Pan Group, Inc.

3. The Florida City transit center housed young women and girls, who had a strong sense of camaraderie. By permission of Operation Pedro Pan Group, Inc.

4. Near the end of the rescue operation, Cuban boys move to the barracks at Opa-Locka airport. By permission of Operation Pedro Pan Group, Inc.

5. George Guarch was Mister Rescue to the lone, often scared youngsters arriving at Miami International Airport. By permission of Operation Pedro Pan Group, Inc.

6. Pedro Pan children at the Miami airport, 1961. By permission of Operation Pedro Pan Group, Inc.

7. Above: High school graduates, San Raphael's, 1963, with Father Bryan Walsh (also shown here). By permission of Operation Pedro Pan Group, Inc.

8. Left: Sara Yaballi, Matecumbe nurse–"Aunt Sara," received hundreds of letters from boys after they left Miami. Photograph by the author.

School. Diplomas were granted in 1963.[33] The school was accredited by Dade County, administered by the Diocese of Miami, and staffed by Cuban American teachers. Classes were conducted in English. After one school year, however, it was clear that it was more cost effective and better socially for the boys to attend local schools. In June 1964 the remaining Matecumbe boys were moved to the same Opa-Locka facility as the former Kendall residents.[34]

The Florida City transit center, several miles south of Miami, consisted of large garden-style apartments. How the buildings came to be used by the Catholic Welfare Bureau is a reflection of Walsh's imagination. Father Walsh had served as pastor of Sacred Heart Parish, near Florida City, before being assigned to head the Catholic Welfare Bureau. Even after his reassignment, despite the long drive, Walsh continued to see the same dentist in the Florida City area. After one dental visit, while the Cuban Children's Program was still in its infancy yet the Kendall facility was bursting at its seams, Walsh explored the area in his car, looking for possible facilities for girls and young boys. Surprisingly, a group of modern apartment buildings appeared empty. Walsh found that they belonged to Mayor Navilio of Florida City, whom Walsh knew personally, and the two men struck a mutually beneficial agreement. After the mayor agreed to build a dining room and a fence, the Catholic Welfare Bureau leased the apartment complex—giving Walsh his desperately needed space and saving Navilio from bankruptcy.[35]

Florida City became the most populous of the Miami centers, housing at its peak up to five hundred children: girls of all ages and boys to the age of twelve. Typically, Florida City's children often relocated to other parts of the United States, yet the facility had a homelike atmosphere. Cuban couples acted as houseparents, and the administrator was a Cuban cleric—Father Salvador de Cisterna, O.F.M., Cap. Father Cisterna was assisted by six sisters of St. Philip Neri who had operated schools in Cuba and by several Cuban American staff members, in the same roles as those at Matecumbe and Kendall.[36]

Consistent with the other camps, Florida City had a permissive atmosphere. Its structured and supervised activities included picnics and trips to the beach. In order to maintain at least a hint of normal social life in such abnormal circumstances, there were frequent dance parties with teenage boys from Matecumbe and the permanent Miami homes (discussed later).

Tents were set up for movies, mass, and shows put on by the children. Because of its unique setup, Florida City offered an opportunity for its young women to act as role models for the children. Florida City's older children attended local schools in Homestead, and the younger ones were schooled at the center itself.[37]

As at Matecumbe and Kendall, Florida City's population shrank after the end of Operation Pedro Pan, especially when the Freedom Flights began in 1965, and children were reunited with their parents in large numbers. Florida City closed in 1965, and its remaining children moved to a home near U.S. Highway 1, under the supervision of the Portos, Cuban houseparents.[38]

The Catholic Welfare Bureau met all the children's basic needs when they passed through the three transit centers. Father Walsh hired Crotty Brothers of Boston to provide food service at a remarkably low price. The arrangement was one of many that at first glance seemed insignificant but that were a key to the program's success. Medical professionals from the centers' well-equipped, modern infirmaries saw to the children's health. Under the Dade County Health Department's supervision, the infirmary nurses, mostly Cuban, provided care in times of illness and inoculations against communicable diseases. The overcrowding at the centers made such measures indispensable.[39]

While the Catholic Welfare Bureau staff desperately sought placements for the children housed in the transit centers, the bureau also established two permanent group care homes in Miami, both for teenage boys. The purpose of the homes, particularly during the program's hectic period, was twofold. The first purpose was to fill the void created by the reluctance of outside agencies to accept teenage boys. Second, the two Miami homes served as showcases for visiting welfare workers from other dioceses, in the hope that visitors would establish similar facilities to house Cuban boys awaiting relocation in Matecumbe and Kendall.

Unlike the transit centers, the permanent homes were not segregated from the rest of the community, being located instead in residential areas. The resident boys lived with the same freedom as American teenagers. They were able to work part-time, and they came and went as they pleased within certain guidelines. They attended local private and public schools. Recreational activities at the homes included television, basketball, Ping-Pong, trips to the beach, and weekend excursions.[40]

The first of the Miami permanent group care homes was known by a variety of names: the Ferre House, Casa Carrion, the Cuban Boys Home, and its official name: St. Raphael's. Located at 175 S.E. 15th Road, across the street from Assumption Academy, it was the first home used by Walsh. It was donated by Maurice Ferre.

At the beginning of Operation Pedro Pan and the Cuban Children's Program, St. Raphael's served as a reception center for boys. It took on its role as a permanent home when Operation Pedro Pan tidal-waved in subsequent months and the other facilities were opened as transit centers. In January 1961, when Angel Carrion became resident housefather (later his wife Nina served as housemother), St. Raphael's was unofficially christened Casa Carrion by the boys. At one point James Baker served briefly as a housefather there when he arrived from Cuba.

St. Raphael's in 1962 had eighty boys in residence. A small handful of them had been sent back from other parts of the country by caretakers with whom the boys had trouble. Father Walsh himself was the head of the home and established his permanent residence there. The main building was a large, apartment-style structure that surrounded a courtyard. Adjacent to it, another structure contained chapel and dining facilities. St. Raphael's was closed around the same time as Matecumbe, and its residents also moved to Opa-Locka.[41]

The other permanent Miami home, the Jesuit Boys Home, was administered by Cuban Jesuit priests. Often referred to as Whitehall, it housed approximately forty teenage boys who attended the newly founded Belen Jesuit Preparatory School in Miami. Belen was originally located in Havana, where it was Cuba's premier school for boys. It was closed by the Castro government in 1961, and the Jesuits were subsequently expelled from Cuba. Ironically, Belen's most famous graduate was Fidel Castro himself.

The Jesuits reopened their school in Miami during the early 1960s, first in rented space at Gesu Parish. Later, the school moved to a former warehouse on Southwest 8th Street, where it remained until the early 1980s. One of the most intriguing Cuban exile institutions, Belen in South Florida conducted classes in English. By the end of the century, Belen had become one of the region's most highly regarded academic institutions. From its sprawling, modern, western Dade County campus, opened in the early 1980s, the school taught many Cuban American boys whose fathers, grandfathers, and great-grandfathers had attended the school in Cuba. Although retaining much of its Cuban and Spanish flavor, Belen became more thoroughly Americanized as generations of Cuban Americans born in the United States filled its halls. The Jesuit Boys Home and Belen's early history in the United States were thus intertwined. The Jesuit Boys Home closed its doors along with St. Raphael's and Matecumbe in 1964, and its remaining residents were transferred to Opa-Locka.[42]

The Cuban Children's Program had thus entered a new phase by 1964, when the boys from Kendall, Matecumbe, Whitehall, and St. Raphael's had all moved to the U.S. Marine barracks at the Opa-Locka airport. Administered eventually by the Jesuits and a small staff of cooks and houseparents, Opa-Locka was comfortable, the barracks being large and airy.[43] It was not a transit center, since the number of children arriving from Cuba was reduced to a slow trickle, and there was no longer a need to place them in foster care or move them to other parts of the country.

In 1965 Cuba and the United States signed a memorandum of understanding that initiated the Freedom Flights. Parents of children who had arrived unaccompanied were among those given priority on the flights. During the airlift's early stages, children under care in Miami and elsewhere were reunited with their parents in massive numbers. Thus, although still accepting unaccompanied children brought to the attention of the Catholic Welfare Bureau, the number of children in the Cuban Children's Program was reduced even further.

By mid-1966, only five hundred children nationwide were still in the Cuban Children's Program.[44] Only a small percentage were still being housed at the Miami centers, and large facilities such as Opa-Locka were unnecessary. In the summer of 1966, the boys were moved to a home on Southwest 8th Street and Brickell Avenue in Miami, under the care of houseparents and a single Jesuit priest—Luis Ripoll.[45] Ripoll was an extraordinary figure whose skills at ministering to teenage boys were legendary. Generations of Cuban men, in both Cuba and the United States, have fond memories of Ripoll as a counselor and a friend.

The remaining boys were moved once again in September 1970—this time to its final location, a small building once used as a hotel on Biscayne Boulevard and 114th Street in Miami Shores; at no time did it contain more than thirty boys. In 1981 the Cuban Children's Program officially ended. The girls and boys near U.S. Highway 1 remained at that home until

1981. Walsh, whose fallback plan was eventually to use the Archdiocese of Miami's homes for dependent children, carefully arranged that all of the children would have reached the age of eighteen by the time the Cuban Children's Program's homes were closed. Thus no children had to enter the fallback facilities. By 1981, of course, all of the Pedro Pan children had long since grown into adulthood, and the Cuban Children's Program's population represented those who left Cuba unaccompanied long after Operation Pedro Pan had ceased.[46]

Finding New Homes

Before the Cuban missile crisis ended Operation Pedro Pan and the mass exodus, the Catholic Welfare Bureau's primary objective was to move children from the Miami centers to permanent foster care–type arrangements, if possible in Miami with other Cubans.[47] But as the number of Cuban children grew into the thousands, Walsh had to call upon the National Conference of Catholic Charities and Catholic dioceses throughout the United States for help. Children in transit centers were sometimes forced to share beds with siblings or sleep on the floor, and Walsh had to worry that several hundred more children might be arriving within hours.

Taking advantage of ninety-five child-care agencies in more than thirty-five states, the Catholic Welfare Bureau placed nearly 6,500 children.[48] The out-of-Miami placements included Catholic foster families, Catholic child-care facilities (with parts sectioned off for Cuban children), Catholic orphanages, and Catholic group homes established especially for the Cuban Children's Program and often administered by clerical and lay Cuban adults. Boarding schools, although used, were not the preferred means of care, as they could not meet the necessities of year-round or total care.

Even for children placed outside Miami, Father Walsh and the Catholic Welfare Bureau of the Diocese of Miami remained responsible, and the bureau kept tight reins on cooperating agencies. Receiving agencies had to be licensed by state welfare departments. In addition, Walsh formulated contracts between the Catholic Welfare Bureau and the receiving agencies, outlining the details of the financial arrangements with the Children's Bureau and the stipulations for minimum standards of care. The Catholic Welfare Bureau also kept a day-to-day record at its Reception and Placement Center of the children's locations and whatever changes occurred. Regular inspection visits were made by the Catholic Welfare Bureau staff and seemingly valid complaints were followed up, particularly in group home placements.[49]

From the beginning Walsh knew he could fall back on Catholic agencies throughout the United States if the number of children grew too numerous to be placed in Miami.[50] The nucleus for planning was a series of meetings in early 1961 with Catholic Relief Services and its director, Bishop Edward Swanstrom.[51] An April 1962 meeting gave further impetus to creating the national network. Details of the Cuban Children's Program had become public in March 1962, through a story in the *Cleveland Plain Dealer*. Walsh had little choice but to issue a press release in response. In it, Walsh deliberately omitted any mention of Operation Pedro Pan.[52] Nevertheless, the incident allowed the Catholic Welfare Bureau to use certain publicity, withheld until that point in the interest of discretion, to seek foster care.

The Catholic Welfare Bureau was able to find places for so many children partly because existing Catholic child care agencies stepped forward at the request of Catholic Charities. Sometimes a single notice in a church bulletin was enough to draw many foster home offers. When appeals went out in a more open fashion after the program was made public in March 1962, HEW Secretary Ribicoff publicly asked American families for help.[53] Pleas were also made through various media, including religious publications. For example, an article in the *Christian Century* sought foster families:

> About 300 Cuban children arrive in this country unaccompanied by their parents [daily]. In whatever way they can many Cuban parents who cannot leave the island themselves are sending their children to the States to protect them from the hardships which are falling upon the Cuban people under the Castro regime and to prevent their forced indoctrination in communism in the Cuban public schools. ... Many U.S. citizens traveling through Latin America have received the gracious Spanish welcome, "esta es su casa." Now several hundred American families can return the hospitality each month, saying to Cuban children bereft of parents, "Make yourself at home." Under the Cuban Refugee Program the Department of Health, Education, and Welfare will pay for the care of the children. But homes are needed. We can think of few better ways to "fight communism" than to care for the children who flee from it.[54]

Many families willing to help did not meet state requirements for child care provision. Even so, references to the cold war and appeals to the sense of Christian generosity had the desired effect, as benevolent volunteers came forward from around the country.

Inviting Catholic welfare agency directors from other regions to experience the refugee situation firsthand also proved effective. When the directors saw the transit centers and the permanent homes in Miami they were often inspired. Some took children back to their own dioceses for group or foster family care, even in cases when they were specifically told not to do so by their superiors. In other cases, dioceses offered the use of vacant facilities. Many of them were eventually used to house children and were manned by adult Cuban laity and clergy. One such diocese was that in Albuquerque, which offered to open a group home facility for Cuban boys, a haven for difficult-to-place teenagers. The home opened in June 1962 and was operated by Marist Brothers from Cuba.[55]

The most responsive dioceses were usually the smallest. In fact, a disproportionate number of children were relocated to dioceses in the western states. Places such as Albuquerque; Yakima, Washington; and Helena, Montana, were among the most responsive. That would seem odd on the surface, since those areas were more sparsely populated and contained far fewer Catholics than northeastern and midwestern cities. A closer look yields an answer. In the first place, dioceses in large industrial cities already had overwhelming caseloads of dependent children.[56] In fact, the placements that didn't work out usually seemed to be cities such as Brooklyn, Philadelphia, and industrial areas in New Jersey. As early as 1961, New Jersey in particular had a bad reputation in Camp Matecumbe.[57] Another reason was that homes in the West were larger and better suited for foster care.[58]

Transporting children to their new locations was also a highly regulated affair. In fact, the Catholic Welfare Bureau even formed a special unit to deal exclusively with that responsibility. First of all, airline officials were always made aware of whom they were transporting. Also, a special code system was developed so that the receiving agent at an airport could prove his or her authenticity. To Walsh's credit, not one child was lost or harmed during the entire enterprise.[59] Considering that the passengers were thousands of non-English-speaking children who had never before traveled alone, the accomplishment was impressive.

The psychological impact on children sent out of Miami was significant. Clearly, they suffered more trauma than those who remained in South Florida. One former Matecumbe teacher called it a "double exile," since children who had already experienced a wrenching separation were suddenly forced to adapt to a second new situation, this time in a completely alien culture.[60] At the Miami transit centers, the children were at least around other Cuban children and usually under the supervision of Cuban adults in the same predicament. In that atmosphere, although geographically abnormal, familiar cultural norms prevailed.

When taken away from the familiar Cuban environment and placed in, say, Helena, Montana, children experienced culture shock in addition to the pain of being separated from their families.[61] Nor was Father Walsh insensitive to the problem. He never asked any child under his direct care to assimilate at a pace faster than that set by the child himself or herself.[62] Nevertheless, given the overcrowded conditions at the Miami centers and the general spirit of relocation that existed among government officials in the early 1960s, Walsh had no choice. He had to relocate children in whatever appropriate Catholic foster care arrangement he could find. In some cases, program officials even went to the trouble of finding local Cuban families where the children had been placed so that they could visit the youngsters and make them feel more comfortable.[63]

The additional trauma experienced by children sent away from Miami was unavoidable. What made matters worse was that a disproportionate number of girls and young boys were moved because of the preferences of child care providers. Cuban girls, having lived extremely sheltered lives compared to their American counterparts, were generally unprepared for the entire experience. Young children, although more adaptable than the older ones, were less able to understand their situation at an intellectual level. As far as they could tell, they were first sent away by their parents and then later by others whom they had grown to trust. In spite of their ordeal, most children adapted remarkably well.

Seven

A Watershed Experience:
Torn from Family, All Alone,
Rescued in Miami

I felt like I was dropped.
Daniel Merida

Years after the event, most of Operation Pedro Pan's 14,048 children remembered the exact date and time of day of their arrival in the United
States, an indication that their journey and subsequent experience marked
a watershed event in their lives. Being torn from the safety of their homes
and suddenly finding themselves alone were both traumatizing and char-
acter-building experiences.

The children's experiences varied. The greatest factors in measuring the
extent of trauma or suffering were age, type and location of placement, and
the amount of time a child spent separated from his or her family. The
experience of separation compounded the trauma normally associated
with being refugees.

Because the children came mostly from middle-class families, their
former economic comfort and close sense of family had a strong impact on
those who entered foster care.[1] First of all, it made them atypical participants in a welfare program, welfare workers noted. Moreover, many had to
make wrenching efforts to adapt, since most of them had never been separated from their families for such an extended period of time. Their former

overprotection was likewise noted by more than one observer.[2] Also, many children were somewhat confused. Because most of them thought they were going to the United States to attend school for a few months (a common practice among some middle- to upper-class Cubans before the revolution), some were shocked to find themselves packed into over-crowded camps in the wilderness. Those sent away from Miami were further surprised when they moved in with foster families. Because the concept of a foster family did not exist in Cuba, the experience was unnerving for many. Children who experienced poor placements, such as those sent to orphanages, suffered even more. A small handful of them were, in fact, placed in schools, usually Catholic boarding schools, in different parts of the United States.

Among the several stages that made up the experience of Pedro Pan children and those who also entered the Cuban Children's Program, patterns were easily discernible. The various stages, described as much as possible in the words of those who lived the experience, are the subject of this and the following chapter.

The use of testimonies is not intended as an exercise in anecdotal history. Instead, the eyewitness accounts are a means of presenting the reality of what the children lived through and their impressions of the experience. Some of those interviewed had given their experience a good deal of thought during the years between participating in the programs and being interviewed for this book. Others spoke of it for the first time in more than thirty years.

For many Pedro Pan participants, the experience began when they were first told they would be traveling to the United States without their parents. The reactions, quite naturally, were mixed. Most children (as well as their parents) believed they were going away for only a short while and would soon be reunited in Cuba. Deep down, however, many seemed to harbor a profound sense of doom. Somehow, the pretense of visiting the United States for a few months of study abroad was undermined by a reality they knew only too well. Most were aware they were being sent away to escape the firing line while Cuba's fate was determined. Most also understood they were being protected from forced Communist indoctrination. They realized that their world had been turned upside down. Schools had been or were threatened with being closed. Many young people sent away after the spring of 1961 had been kept from attending state schools, being secretly tutored at home. Many had seen their parents' businesses, or the businesses for which they worked, confiscated. A number of them had relatives in political prisons or in exile. That many were told to keep their departure a secret from friends, neighbors, and even other relatives only furthered their awareness of the situation's seriousness.

The thought of being separated from their parents was frightful for most children, whereas the prospect of travel and riding in an airplane for the first time was a source of great excitement for some. For those who saw beyond the airplane ride and truly grasped the reality of separation, however, a sense of dread was inescapable. One such person, who preferred anonymity, was the daughter of a prominent Havana architect, the eldest of seven brothers and sisters. She and three younger siblings were among the first children sent out of Cuba through Operation Pedro Pan. They were also among the first placed outside Miami through the Cuban Children's Program. She was only eleven years old when she left Cuba on January 20, 1961. She remembered vividly being told by her parents that she would be leaving Cuba and what occurred in the weeks preceding her departure:

> I went to an American school. The Merici nuns were American Ursuline nuns and they were expelled. They offered to take us out. . . . My father and then the family, after thinking about the matter decided to do it because they were afraid. They were told that [if we stayed] we would be taken to centers of indoctrination, to be separated from our families, and to be brainwashed. So they agreed to let us go. The nuns would arrange for us to leave. So the nuns left, and [my parents] set about preparing us for the trip. . . . I was eleven, my sister —— was nine, —— was eight, and —— was six years old. . . . They got us visa waivers for Jamaica. . . . The worst Christmas of my life was the Christmas before we left Cuba because we knew the inevitable was coming. That year [for the first time] I knew everything I was getting [as a Christmas gift]—everything was functional for the trip. It was the first year I stayed up with the adults and put the gifts out. I begged and begged, "Please don't make me go, please don't make me go," and they made me go.[3]

Maria Teresa Carrera left Cuba on September 12, 1961. Before the revolution, her family was involved in agricultural enterprises in Sancti

Espiritus, Las Villas Province. A sheltered life and attendance at the local Catholic school for girls was the nine-years-old's background when she left Cuba on Operation Pedro Pan. She remembered being told that she and her brother would be traveling to the United States without her parents. Her story is typical of Pedro Pan children:

> They told me that we had to go and that they would be joining us as soon as they could—even thinking about it makes me cry—I didn't even realize what was going to happen. I thought because we were going to all these government agencies and all this, I thought that [my parents] would be coming along right behind us. [We] were separated [just] under two years. . . . Now that I have my own children, I think that they [my parents] were very brave, that they thought there was this desperate situation in Cuba that they were going to lose their children and that they would rather lose them to democracy where they could have a future than to Communism.[4]

The moment of truth for virtually all the children came during the tense moments just prior to their departure. Havana's international airport was a modern facility by the day's standards. In it was a glass-enclosed area nicknamed *la pecera* (the fishtank), where travelers gathered to await departure. Most devastating for the Pedro Pan children, only passengers were allowed beyond la pecera's entrance, and the children were separated by the glass walls from those they loved. It was inside la pesera that many Pedro Pan children truly absorbed the enormity and the seriousness of what was happening. Cut off from their parents' touch, yet able to see them, made being in la pecera one of the Pedro Pan children's most vivid and haunting memories. Many suddenly felt it was the last time they would see their parents.

Although most were ultimately reunited, it was through la pecera's glass walls that some parents saw their offspring as children for the last time. For a number of the youngsters, that last moment of seeing their parents through the eyes of childhood was the final sight of them. Carlos Alamilla recalled, "I remember that very vividly, because that's the last time I saw my father. I had a very strong intuition at that time that I would never see him again."[5] For many children, la pecera also represented the threshold between their accustomed security and protection at home and a world of loneliness, disorientation, and cultural adaptation.

In la pecera the children, no matter how young, were left on their own to deal with airport officials. Although most Pedro Pan children were not harassed, they were not treated with the kindness a frightened child would usually evoke. After all, the children were abandoning the revolution—airport officials knew this. In many cases the young travelers were forced to leave behind clothing, jewelry, dolls, and other personal belongings in accordance with the stringent requirements placed on those traveling abroad. They were searched, and any possessions beyond the limit of approximately three sets of clothes were confiscated. Terrified, their parents helpless, the children usually complied with the officials. Daniel Merida remembered his feelings inside la pesera:

It was kind of exciting to know that I was going to take a plane . . . [but] my father was like freaking out. . . . Then, I'm in the pesera. That's when I stopped, when everything became real for me because it was a feeling that I lost my independence, I lost control. For the first time in my life I knew—it was like being in jail—I was not going to be allowed to do certain things, period. I couldn't talk. The first thing that happened to me was that I was in line, and [a Cuban airport official] came to me and told me—I had a watch, I had a ring, and I had a gold chain, and I think I remember having a bracelet with my name on it, it was all gold—and the guy said to me, "You can't take gold out of the country, so give it to me." So I looked at my father. I walked away from this guy telling me to take my things off. I went up to the glass and I told my father, and my father was crying. That's what really freaked me out, that my father was crying and—if I think about it now, it can make me cry. My father was crying and he was saying to me, really loud, "Give him the gold!" And I kept saying to him, "But it's mine!" He kept saying "Give it to him!". . . I think that's the first time it really hit me, that this is something really weird, that I'm leaving and I'm not going to see him tomorrow. This is not a joke any more . . . this is when it became more real for me. When I saw my father crying, my mother crying, and all these other guys that were there were feeling really bad.[6]

He later added:

It was scary because it felt cold. It felt naked. . . . These people were looking at you, and they were looking at you in a very different way.

You didn't know if you were going to come out of there alive. For the first time in my life my father cannot help me. He is one foot away from me [behind the glass], and I'm telling him, "They are taking this from me" and he's saying to me "Give it to them." *He* gave it [the gold jewelry] to me. *He* bought it for me. Why am I giving it to this *asshole?* My father and mother kept telling me they loved me, they loved me, that they, [gasp]—that's the way it was. It was very dramatic.[7]

Aurora Candelaria was thirteen when she left Cuba with her older sister, Lourdes. She recalled her departure from Cuba on October 3, 1961: "I got by the airplane and saw my mother outside la pecera, that's when it hit me. . . . I said 'Oh, my God, what is going to happen here now?' My sister was more independent, but I was more dependent, I was the youngest too. Then I started crying while I was going into the airplane and I saw my mother, my uncle, and aunt, and then that was when it hit."[8]

Teresa Ponte was one of the many children tutored at home after the closure of private schools. She recalled her experience at Havana's airport: "I was harassed, [as] a nine-year-old could be harassed, in the sense that they insisted on taking the dolls that I was carrying with me, they insisted on taking the little pieces of jewelry that I was wearing, which was probably earrings, because I didn't wear any jewelry, probably just little earrings. They insisted on [taking]—I remember this very clearly, I think my parents had given me or I had gotten from somewhere—coins, like a nickel or a dime. They made me give that up."[9]

The actual departure and ride to Miami seemed, in many cases, to be worse than the pesera experience. Some children blocked the experience from their memories completely. Daniel Merida did not. He said of the flight: "I remember walking to the plane, because you walked to the plane at that time, and it was scary. I thought my legs were trembling a little bit, I felt kind of funny. Then I sat on the plane. . . . They gave me something to drink, I guess it was Coke. Then halfway to Miami the man in the plane said, 'You are now over American waters,' and everybody started screaming, 'Yay!'. . . I wasn't screaming. People were saying, 'We're free!'"[10]

The eleven-year-old child mentioned earlier, in charge of three younger siblings, took a flight headed for Jamaica with a layover in Miami. The four were to disembark when they reached Miami. The woman she became told of the experience: "There were two older boys, or three boys, that were like fifteen or sixteen, you know, and I saw they were so old, and they were going to be traveling with us and I was kind of relieved. I don't remember the flight at all. I remember being very scared about where my sister went, what she did, who she talked to, feeling that I had to protect her. My sister ——, she was having a ball. She and —— thought it was a vacation. I was scared."[11]

Elisa Vilano-Chovel was from Guanabacoa, just outside Havana. Her father, a certified public accountant, and her mother decided to send her and her sister to the United States after a teenage cousin was imprisoned by the Castro regime. Also, as in many cases, the girls were sent away out of a general fear of Communist indoctrination and the loss of *patria potestad*. She recalled her experience:

> I will tell you sincerely that I had a panicking fear. I had never even taken a bus by myself. Then what happened was that I—knowing my sister was more given to fear than me—I wasn't going to demonstrate to my sister that I was dying of fear. Then the stewardess came and offered us Coca-Cola. Then I was heartbroken because we didn't see my mother with the umbrella. We were seated on the other side of the airplane. My mother had told us, "When you are out there [on the plane], I'm going to have a red umbrella so that [you can see me]." Imagine what sadness. We were looking for the umbrella and not seeing it because she was on the other side. That's pathetic.[12]

The issue of older siblings protecting their younger brothers and sisters was a poignant and powerful one. The concept of protection is a recurring theme in the remainder of this book. Psychologist Lourdes Rodriguez wrote her doctoral dissertation at Boston University on the psychological effects of parental separation on unaccompanied children. A child of Pedro Pan herself, she studied other Pedro Pan women as her subjects. Rodriguez detailed the impact of their experience on their lives and emphasized the role of caretaker as being critically important. Rodriguez argued that taking care of younger siblings gave older brothers and sisters a purpose and an expectation to live up to.[13] Here, the two preceding statements by Cubans support that theory. Other examples are cited in the discussion of the children's experience in the United States.

When the Catholic Welfare Bureau awaited the Cuban children in Miami, the process of picking them up and dealing with procedures at the airport changed little throughout the program. At no time did anyone know how many children would arrive on any given day. The bureau nevertheless prepared to accept whatever number arrived. After Walsh waited for the children himself during the program's first few days, Louise Cooper was assigned to the daily airport vigil. Within weeks, James Baker assumed the role. For a time in early 1961, Margarita Oteiza was in charge of airport details and transportation to the camps.[14] She recalled:

> The children arrived at whatever time of day or night, or afternoon. They informed Mr. Baker and then, in the beginning I went myself, but when that grew, that the amount arriving was too much, I had to arrange a group of volunteers. Don't forget the Cubans who arrived here during that time, the cars we had, what we called transportation, were a poor excuse for a car. But they functioned. So I would call my volunteers with their fleet of destroyed cars. I would call and say, "Hey, five or six are arriving. You go here, You go there," then they'd convene at the airport and picked up the children.[15]

By mid-1961 the airport process crystallized into its final form. That was when George Guarch, described by the *New York Times* as a "tall, dour Cuban-American, once in the Havana export business," took charge of meeting the children, having their paperwork processed, and transporting them to the camps. Guarch was praised by airport employees for his dedication. His reputation with news reporters, on the other hand, suffered. While undoubtedly protecting the semisecret nature of Operation Pedro Pan, he "smashed news photographers' cameras."[16] George Guarch, although not known personally to the children or their parents in Cuba, was nevertheless the person many children were told to ask for when they reached Miami.[17]

Guarch tried to make the children feel as comfortable as possible, often distributing candy and bubble gum while checking their papers. After a flight's arrival, he first united children with relatives or friends waiting at the airport to take them under care, thus ending their experience as unaccompanied refugees. He then gathered the unclaimed. Any Jewish child among them was given over to the United HIAS official at the airport. Protestant children were usually taken to a Catholic Welfare Bureau transit center, which arranged for the Children's Service Bureau to take over as soon as possible. In any case, after a short speech about how their behavior while guests in the United States would reflect upon Cuba, Guarch piled the children into a large station wagon and took them to the transit centers.[18] He often took children to stay with his own family when the camps overflowed.

Guarch secretly kept a log of the children who arrived in Miami. In the interests of both discretion and security, he should not have done so, yet family inquiries as to the safe arrival of their children were such that he kept a record anyway. The log did not surface until his death in June 1991.[19]

When the children arrived in Miami, they were both bewildered and frightened—the comfort Guarch offered notwithstanding. Aurora Candelaria vaguely remembered her first moments in the United States: "There was a woman who was a good friend of my uncle and aunt who was waiting there for us. But they told us, 'All the children who came alone line up over here,' so my cousin, my sister, and I queued up. But my cousin was another nucleus. So my cousin, because he was a boy, was taken to Matecumbe. Then my sister and I went to Kendall."[20]

Martin Ling and his younger brother were thrown into a confused state when they arrived. They expected to meet a priest who was a family friend. When the priest did not appear, the boys panicked. They were put into the group of the unclaimed and ushered by strangers into a vehicle. They had no idea what was happening. Ling remembered:

There was such uncertainty there: "What do we do here?". . . That night I found [Guarch] to be a serious person, kind of businesslike. He gave us gum, Coca-Cola, but, you know, "Where are they taking us?" We got into the van, and the distance from the airport to Camp Matecumbe was like going to the ends of the earth. . . . We only learned [at the airport] that we were leaving with George. But of course we spoke to the other boys also to see what was going on: "Are you leaving too?" We were about six or seven in the group. In the group there was a little more comfort.[21]

Inevitably, there were amusing episodes of culture shock when the children arrived at Miami International Airport. Armando Codina remembered that all he knew how to say in English was "hamburger and Coke."[22]

Daniel Merida was not the first Cuban refugee, and certainly not the first immigrant, to marvel at the peel-back, pop-out-style American milk carton. He recalled:

> When I got off at the airport in Miami, they gave me a carton of milk. I never saw that in my life. . . . I looked at it, and, I go, I knew it was milk because I knew enough English to know that milk was *leche*. But, how the hell do you open this thing? I didn't know how to open it. I destroyed the damned thing. I mean there was milk coming everywhere. So I took the damned milk and I threw it in the garbage, and when the guy came—an American guy—he came to me and he told me, "Did you like the milk?" and I said it was delicious. I never drank it. I was so embarrassed."[23]

The journey to and arrival at the camps were as shocking to the children as any other part of their experience. The unusual events that preceded their arrival only hardened the blow. When they stepped out of George Guarch's station wagon or another Catholic Welfare Bureau employee's automobile, they encountered a bizarre and chaotic world. Their first nights were often stressful. Having left their parents and then having been shuffled around by strange people in a strange place took its toll. Margarita Oteiza remembered the emotional condition of many children on their first night:

> They came scared. Do not forget the good-bye in Cuba was difficult, that they were coming to the unknown, to complete strangers, into strange hands. Do not forget that Cuban children were very protected . . . children who lived in their families' bosoms, and these are the families who wanted to save their children. They were families who were more worried than not worried, and [the children] arrived very sad, very scared, very tense. It was very sad picking them up at the airport. . . . It was a sad labor. I remember I would be very saddened seeing them arrive. I remember one day a girl arrived with a sign that read "My name is such and such, please treat me well" attached—she was a little girl—on her dress.[24]

When the children arrived at the camps they were interviewed and registered. In a 1962 documentary film produced by the U.S. Information Agency, *The Lost Apple*, an eight-year-old boy is shown during his initial interview at Florida City. He is asked several questions about his age, health history, academic history, and family background. His expression and mannerism betray a sense of confusion, disorientation, even terror. After showing the boy taking in the camp's atmosphere, which includes children playing, filmmakers capture him alone crying desperately into a pillow. All the while, the narrator explains what was happening in a smooth, melodic voice and accented English. He is obviously directing his words to other children in the same situation. The rest of the film shows the boy adapting to life at Florida City, as well as the stories of other children.[25]

Thus awaiting their fate at the transit centers, some children were headed toward lives in other parts of the country that in the long run proved beneficial and enriching. A few went into difficult, sometimes horrid situations. Some were quickly reunited with their parents and never left Miami. The most fortunate of those who were not quickly reunited went to live with Father Walsh at St. Raphael's or with the Jesuits at Whitehall.

Eight

Toward a Resolution:
Young Refugees' Reactions to Transit Centers
and Placements

Here one feels such a lack of affection. They tell us we are already men, but when I lay down most days I feel like crying, like a child, and ask myself, "How much longer, Lord?"
Jorge to Sara Yaballi, writing from Albuquerque, January 12, 1963

Because the children arrived at one of three transit centers—Matecumbe, Kendall, or Florida City, each of which evolved in distinct stages—the children had varying impressions of the experience. No matter the center, they usually adapted to life there, and most were averse to being relocated.[1] There were several reasons for their reluctance. First was the presence at the centers of Cuban adults with whom many children had developed close emotional ties. Second, the other residents were also Cuban, and cultural familiarity and a sense of camaraderie created a feeling of security. Third, while in Miami they were geographically close to Cuba and their families. Moreover, when their parents left Cuba, Miami was the most likely point of arrival.[2]

Elisa Vilano-Chovel arrived at the Florida City transit center with her younger sister in 1962. They remained at the facility for a few months before relocating to a foster home in Buffalo, New York. She remembered the months after arriving: "We were exposed to so much. There was immense heat. I remember it was so, so hot in Florida City. We used to walk in line to a park that was nearby. . . . There were snakes everywhere, there were bugs. . . . They gave us art classes, they gave us math classes—they kept us busy—exercises. . . . Then they had talent shows on the weekends, they had parties. . . . Later on they also took us to the pool at Matecumbe."[3]

The talent shows and dances Elisa referred to were the center of social life at Florida City. In a scene from the documentary film *The Lost Apple*, Florida City children are shown performing in a talent show for their mates' entertainment. A girl of around twelve ends the show by singing a heartfelt rendition of a Cuban folk song. Her performance has a sobering effect on the formerly playful crowd. Their estrangement from Cuba is brought home once again in the film when a Cuban priest gives a moving, though somewhat stern, speech. He speaks to his young audience of Cuba's "crucial hour" and of their duty to rebuild the fatherland once it is freed. Both the speech and the reaction to it clearly illustrate that the priest's audience believes that its return to Cuba is imminent.[4] They would undoubtedly have been shocked to learn that their presence in Florida City in 1962 was more than a temporary derailment of their regular lives in Cuba. Instead, it was the first moments in their lives as Americans.

Luis Ramudo stayed at the Kendall facility for several weeks before he was transferred to St. Raphael's. Luis witnessed the change at Kendall when the Marist Brothers took over, and remembered his weeks at the facility: "Kendall at first was administered by an American woman . . . but it later came under the Marist Brothers, specifically Brother Maximiliano, who was the director. Brother Maximiliano had been the director of the Marist school in Camagüey, which I attended until the third grade. We knew each other from there. When the Marist Brothers came, they were the ones who initiated classes. We started to study. . . . Before that they were not giving classes and we were in a state of limbo."[5]

A woman who passed through Kendall for three days in early 1961, before being sent to Philadelphia, reported, "We were the first girls to arrive there. . . . We left Cuba on the nineteenth of January 1961 and we arrived here on the twentieth [at] two in the morning. It was the day Kennedy was inaugurated. I remember there were no girls at this camp— we were the first girls. We were on the downstairs floor and the boys were on the upstairs floor. We had a good time there. They were all Cuban kids.

We played, we didn't have to go to school. We were all in the same boat."[6]

Martin Ling, like most other children, was disoriented when he arrived at Matecumbe. His younger brother was with him during the first few days but was later moved to Kendall because of his age. Despite the separation, Martin remembered his two weeks at the camp fondly:

> That night we both went to Matecumbe. . . . Then the next day—or two days later, I do not remember—my brother, who was younger, on the borderline, went to Kendall. [The first] night we slept in the kitchen. There was a dining room but it seemed the kitchen was warmer. . . . The first days I spent on the lookout because of the *novatadas* [initiations by other boys for the newly arrived]. For example, they would make two lines and play *el quemado* [the burned one] with whoever arrived, throw balls at people. The one that was dreadful was when they would tie you up in a chair and throw you in the pool. I tried to avoid it. Nothing happened to me. . . . One thing that bothered me was having to shower outside. Because there were not enough bathrooms and showers, many of us had to bathe in the showers that were outside the pools, which were made just to rinse. . . . I had never bathed in the nude in front of anyone, and in November it is already quite cool.[7]

In spite of the hardships, most children interviewed for this book felt secure at the camps. Although mischievous at times—as evidenced by Ling's reference to the novatadas—they felt protected. Daniel Merida stated, "I felt secure. I knew these were not the people from the *pecera*—they were nice people, they were on my side. We were just acting like little jerks. . . . There was a structure in Matecumbe."[8]

Margarita Oteiza was a teacher at Matecumbe. Previously a member of Ruston Academy's faculty, she remembered Camp Matecumbe's archaic teaching conditions during the program's early months:

> When I would get there in the mornings in my car, which was a jalopy, I brought all the books and even a portable blackboard because there was not even a classroom. . . . They would wait for me from the time they saw the car—I imagine because of the dust—they would start screaming, "Mrs. Oteiza's safari!" And my safari would come when I opened the trunk of the car and they would all come and take out the books. Everything was an event. . . . They had to take

everything to the pine tree with my name hammered onto it, "Mrs. Oteiza." [They sat] in bleachers. . . . When it rained they gave me permission to use the buses. I was able to sit in the driver's seat and look back. Imagine, I would sit in the driver's seat and I turned like this, then I would give my class there until they started to misbehave. . . . It was not a sense of mission. It was a high school like any other with boys of that age.[9]

Adult Cubans often took the children from the transit centers on weekend excursions to the beaches or to parks.[10] Some children also spent weekends with relatives in the area who could not provide for them on a regular basis, or they visited siblings in other camps.

The teenage Cuban boys who received a *beca* at St. Raphael's, Father Walsh's model home in Miami, or at the Jesuit-run Whitehall were among the most fortunate in the Cuban Children's Program. The staff celebrated all their birthdays.[11] Many had part-time jobs.[12] The most fondly remembered experiences were weekend sailing trips with Father Walsh, excursions that sometimes began from Dinner Key Marina in Coconut Grove. Each time, he took a different group.

Luis Ramudo, who was transferred from Kendall to St. Raphael's, recalled his good fortune:

I had the luck of being moved to Casa Carrion. . . . We went to school like any other child who got on a bus, and went to La Salle [a local Catholic high school]—that was my case. . . . We led a relatively normal life. In the afternoon we would return to Casa Carrion, and we played basketball in the basketball court. On the weekends we were able to go downtown. We would go to the movies. I went out with Walsh two or three times. He liked sailing. He would rent a twenty-foot sailboat. Three or four of us would go. He had a Mercedes-Benz then, and all who fit into the Mercedes Benz could go sailing. . . . I had the opportunity to go with him a couple of times.[13]

In spite of the freedom at St. Raphael's, Walsh ruled the home with an iron fist. The rules, although liberal, were strongly enforced. Violations sometimes resulted in paddlings by the priest with the linebacker physique. According to Alfonso Garcia, one of the boys at St. Raphael's,

Then there was the paddle. That was only where Walsh lived. Nobody else could hit the children. . . . So, you would get there with some problem and he let you choose. You had three options: lose part of your allowance—or all of it depending upon your offense—or lose your going-out privileges—part of it or all of it. . . Then there were his six paddles, one was bamboo. . . . Then he would tell you, "Two paddles with the bamboo, four with the wooden, or two with the leather one." It was a joke, you know, but a joke that worked. . . . Discipline existed for sure, but in a kind of silly way. Me, for example, my biggest problems with him was studying. I was not allowed to study at night because he would come to the bathroom and take me out and force me back into bed while paddling me. . . . If you could not do your homework by nine, you would go to bed without doing it.[14]

Boys in Cuba generally began smoking cigarettes at a younger age than in the United States, a cultural difference that gave Father Walsh a difficult time. Garcia recalled his conflict with Walsh over the issue and how it was resolved:

There came a time when there were so many people who smoked that Walsh could not control it. One day he got mad and said, "If you want to smoke, I want a telegram from your parents giving authorization." Imagine that. I spoke to Mother once a week. When I spoke to her that Saturday, I did not know what to tell her, [so I said], "Look Mom, you know one gets nervous here and I smoke a cigarette now and then, but now this priest wants us to have a telegram sent." Imagine my mother. I was alone here, and she was there. If I would have asked her to send a telegram authorizing me to handle nuclear weapons, she would have sent it.[15]

Those who stayed with Walsh regarded him as a great man. Ralph Sanchez, who had become the promoter of the Miami Grand Prix, said of Walsh, "He was a true father to us."[16] Moises Hernandez, a prominent Miami medical doctor who was also one of Walsh's charges, said, "He was very strict about the rules, but at the same time I felt protected. It did me good to know that someone worried about me so much. He loved us all very much."[17] Alfonso Garcia called him a "man of great compassion."[18]

The boys at the Jesuits' Whitehall received similar care. Luis Ripoll, S.J., ultimately took charge of the operation and later of all the Miami boys when the Cuban Children's Program had been reduced to only a handful of youngsters. Ripoll explained in a 1968 interview: "We try to make the boys feel at home. We try to let them know that we love them and are happy they are with us. True, there can be no substitute for a father and mother. But at least we can make them feel someone cares for them while they await a reunion. . . . Our job is twofold. We have to make the boys happy here, but at the same time we have to keep the memory of their parents and of their culture alive."[19]

Thrown Head-First into U.S. Culture

When a child at a transit center learned of his permanent placement, or beca, one of the social workers explained to the child his or her destination, often with the help of a map.[20] For some children, leaving Miami was a wrenching experience, as they lost not only a familiar environment they had just become accustomed to, but also their native culture as they were thrown head-first into U.S. culture. Many others found the experience enriching.

The children were sent to Catholic dioceses in more than thirty-five states and placed in various types of care arrangements (see chapter 6). Because there was consensus among social workers at the time that foster homes were preferable to institutionalized care, the former were used as often as possible.[21] Expectations did not live up to reality in most cases because the Cuban children were sent into environments unfamiliar to them, no matter how well a particular placement ultimately went.

Some children were shocked to find that their becas were in orphanages or homes for neglected and dependent children. Many protested immediately.[22] St. Vincent's Home in Brooklyn, New York, was one such institution. A teenage boy, Regino, wrote in a December 1961 letter from St. Vincent's:

> The food here is garbage, the boys here are Puerto Rican, Italian, American, and black. There is one who upon appearances looks all right, but from what they told me, [though] I am not sure it is true, he was in a juvenile prison and spent some months incarcerated. I do not feel well here, not all of us have the same personality, and I would rather be somewhere else. I do not know if it is that I am a problematic guy, but I will tell you something so that I do not bottle anything up: I do not like this even a little bit. But, what choice do I have? I am resigned to this torture.[23]

It would be easy to accuse young Regino of ingratitude. Yet Regino, like the rest of the children in the Cuban Children's Program, had never before been dependent, neglected, or placed in institutional care. They were separated from their parents temporarily for political reasons. Being sent to a cold, impersonal, reformatory-like institution must have been a considerable shock to Regino. Fortunately, Walsh's staff regularly visited the places where children were sent and in many cases intervened on the Cuban children's behalf or stopped using a facility altogether.[24]

One woman interviewed had been sent to a Philadelphia orphanage, St. Vincent's, run by German American nuns. Although cared for in a material sense, she obviously received the wrong type of placement. She remembered her January 1961 arrival in the city: "They gave us hats, some gloves, and a scarf. I went [with others] to Philadelphia to six feet of snow wearing a Cuban wool suit. It was the most painful thing I've ever experienced in my life. When I got off that plane and I stood there and the wind hit me, [like] I've never, ever felt. . . . It was painful to the bone."

She and her siblings were separated because of their ages and put into different wings of the orphanage. She remembered:

I cried every day for a year. . . . We came from a private school, a very protected childhood. We had nannies to take care of us until we were like ten. All of a sudden I'm in a home where most of the kids were kids that the state would not allow their parents to have. There was one orphan in that school, one girl. Everybody else, their parents were alcoholics, derelicts, prostitutes. Now, I realize that—I didn't realize that then—I just realized that I was old enough to know that was not the atmosphere that we wanted or that we should have been in.

She was ultimately moved to the Cabrini Home, administered by Italian nuns. She said her time there was more pleasant because of the nuns' warmth and loving nature, as well as their ability to make pizza (no doubt also because of greater cultural similarities than with Germans). She nevertheless acknowledged that, although sad and lonely, she was not mistreated by the nuns at St. Vincent's. She believed they did everything possible for her and her siblings.[25]

There were no shortages of poor placements and bad experiences. Yet most placements seem to have gone relatively well. The program's most surprising feature was not the less than ideal situations, but the relatively few inappropriate placements. Finding homes for thousands of children within a span of months was an enormous task. There was no evidence of wide-scale mistreatment, abuse, or neglect—a credit to the Catholic Welfare Bureau's thorough vigilance. In fact, no child—except for three who came from Cuba with chronic health problems—died while in the Cuban Children's Program.[26] Given that thousands of children, many of them teenage boys, were flown to a variety of living situations all around the country, more tragedies would have been expected.

A large number of the former child refugees, perhaps a majority, had fond memories of their caretakers despite the sense of alienation from their families in Cuba. Initially placed in an orphanage, where the pains of her experience included a physical altercation with a nun, Lourdes Borrego, with her sister Aurora Candelaria, then went to live with the Peterson family in Kalispell, Montana. As Lourdes put it, "These Americans were great with us. When we left, they cried."[27] Her sister concurred: "They were a wonderful family, called Monica and Marvin Peterson. They bought us coats; they really treated us as if we were their own children, like part of the family. We called the grandparents Grandma and Grandpa. We were like equals. I cannot tell you that they treated their own children better than they did us."[28]

The girls' relationship with the Petersons grew so close that even after they were reunited with their parents and moved back to Miami, they remained in close contact. Staying in touch with foster parents was common. Many children regularly visited and wrote letters to foster families long after they were discharged from the program, and some continue to do so.

Certain foster family situations went too well. A small handful of children grew so close to their American foster parents during the long separation from their own families that they wanted to remain with the Americans when at long last their Cuban parents arrived in the United States. Similar alienations of familial affections also occurred with some children at the Miami centers.[29] Inevitably, when a child is separated from its natural parents at a young age and spends formative childhood years in a difficult but congenial atmosphere, he or she establishes permanent psychological adjustments. In at least one case a child returned to his foster parents permanently after a short stint with his real parents.[30] Cuban parents who, after a painful separation, suddenly realized that their child did not even recognize them and was incapable of returning their love were profoundly hurt. But such extreme incidents were rare and did not represent any sort of pattern.

Just like experiences in foster family care, placements in other types of care evoked different reactions. A teenage boy wrote in February 1962 from a school in Marquette, Michigan:

> When we arrived, they took us to buy clothes and immediately sent us to a Catholic high school, and we have to study a great deal; and as everything is in English it is much more difficult for us. I feel very good in the high school. The boys and girls treat me very well. I am learning a lot of English. This is marvelous. They give us $2.00 a week, but the only thing we need to spend it on is cigarettes, which is the only thing they do not give us. Everything else they give us in abundance. I have to give God many thanks for having sent me here. We have a good deal of fun here. On Saturdays we go sledding and ski and have snowball fights. All in all, it is a paradise.[31]

A letter from another teenage boy, in Reno, Nevada, tells of a completely opposite experience: "The food is bad, it is not balanced; today they barely turned on the heat, so you can figure the cold there must be. They agreed to buy us clothes and they already ordered it, but it has not been sent. The clothes they have given us [in the meantime] is used; rest assured that this is complete garbage. They have given us things but they rub it in our face all day. There have already been days that they have paddled some of us."[32]

There were cases when tensions flared between Cuban boys sent away together. There were reportedly cliques, usually divided into the religious, the mischievous, and those in between.[33] That classification is supported by some of the letters written to Sara Yaballi, a nurse at Matecumbe. Many boys complained of the behavior of other Cubans.[34]

In any case, children sent outside Miami had to adapt more quickly to American life. Often alone or in small groups, surrounded by an alien culture, they were forced to adapt in even the most basic areas of life. For instance, children experienced an element of shock when they encountered American food. Social workers promptly noticed the problem. Katherine Oettinger, chief of the Children's Bureau, noted, "Diet was one of the most common points of conflict arising from the Cuban child's apparent dislike of everything except meat, black beans, and sugar. The foster parents' expecting them to eat vegetables was the cause of many complaints to [Cuban] parents."[35]

Workers in the Miami homes made a deliberate effort to serve Cuban food, but American foster parents understandably had no such talent. The children had to adapt or starve. A youngster sent to Brooklyn, New York, although not dissatisfied overall, nevertheless stated, "The only thing bad here is the food. There is no one who could eat it, because it is poor in quality and preparation."[36]

Another area of stress concerned chores. Children helped with housework in many middle-class American homes, but no such custom existed in Cuba. The issue of chores thus was sometimes a conflict that had to be resolved through cultural understanding. Some Cuban children sensed exploitation when asked to take out the garbage or help with house-cleaning. A few believed that the home that taken them in had the secret motive of using them as slaves. While not an unknown phenomenon in foster family situations, it was clearly not the intention of most American foster families to secure free domestic service by taking in a Cuban child.

The worst conflicts about chores seemed to arise from boys in general, and teenage boys in particular. Because of their exalted position in the home, Cuban males were shocked when asked to help around the house.[37] Some teenage boys were ignorant of the foster family concept altogether. They viewed their foster homes as boarding arrangements and resisted the authority of the adults under whose care they were placed.[38] Being asked to do chores under such conflicting perceptions often worsened the situation. Nevertheless, many children took chores in stride and understood the situation.[39] Elisa Vilano-Chovel remembered doing chores in her foster family's home as a "welcome shock." She learned to do many things that proved useful to her later.[40] Some other children were asked to do little if any work around the home.

Amid the pain of separation and the frustration of coping with a new language and culture, many Cuban children sent away from Miami were nevertheless enriched culturally. Immersed in the U.S. milieu, they learned to survive and in the process had unique experiences. Elisa Vilano-Chovel, like most Cuban girls, was restricted from physical contact with males before marriage. She remembered her first dance at Bishop Newman High School, where it was "semidark, and they had the strobe. A boy came to dance with me and put his body [close] and his cheek next to my cheek and I thought, 'What a shameless person!' It was a cheek-to-cheek dance and I said, 'What is this?' I was in a state of shock because in Cuba you danced separated."[41]

Taking part in the new culture, Maria Teresa Carrera became a cheerleader, and Daniel Merida learned to dance the twist.[42] Others, such as the teenager Hector, who was placed in Montana, had the opportunity to travel. Hector wrote of how excited he was by a visit to Yellowstone National Park.[43]

Coming from a tropical island with mild year-round temperatures, many children reacted strongly to the unfamiliar weather patterns in places such as Michigan, Montana, Washington, and New York. The cold and snowy winters in such locations were a source of both excitement and depression. One boy wrote from Louisville, Kentucky, "It snowed here for the second time on December 9th, and it snowed a great deal. We walked and buried ourselves in the snow up to our knees, and we also had a snowball fight against the Americans and built snowmen."[44] A boy placed in Brooklyn, New York, remembered his first snowfall as a "beautiful impression."[45] Not all experiences with snow and freezing weather were so pleasing. As Maria Teresa Carrera remembered, in vivid terms, "It was very hard because it was very, very cold. We got there in October, at the end of October. We used to have to walk to school. Many times when I came home for a tomato soup and a cheese-melt sandwich, my legs and my thighs were frozen—I was wearing the coat my mother had made for me in Cuba."[46]

Good Report Cards

In general, the comportment of the Cuban children was excellent, coming as they did from tight-knit homes formerly blessed with economic security. The tensions with their foster families came not so much from a clash of values but from differences in customs. Children who came from dysfunctional homes in Cuba were the only identifiable group that caused major problems.[47]

Katherine Oettinger and John F. Thomas reported on "the strong desire of these children to please their parents and supervisors."[48] They also wrote of their politeness and conformity.[49] The children, in fact, had the reputation of being well behaved, good-natured, law-abiding, and often highly intelligent.[50] As one contemporary observer wrote, they "delighted their caretakers with their politeness, irritated them with their noisy chatter, enraged them with their untidiness, impressed them with their respect for their parents' wishes, and won them with their charm."[51]

Juvenile delinquency among the children was nearly nonexistent, and the number of out-of-wedlock births negligible. Katherine Oettinger and John F. Thomas reported that the Cuban children's gregariousness, noisiness, and volubility were a source of tension with some foster parents but that in most cases tension was resolved through tolerance and understanding by the foster families and behavioral adjustments by the children. Another source of tension was the children's tendency to defer to their parents' authority in Cuba even when it conflicted with the wishes of their foster parents in the United States.[52]

One seemingly insignificant point of contention brought to light by caseworkers was the children's aversion to dentists. Attempting to shield them from pain, many Cuban parents had neglected their children's dental work.[53] Like the other problems, the dental issue was worked out successfully.

Some children especially felt the need to excel while separated from their parents, to prove themselves to themselves, their parents, and the Americans. They said that they had not only tried to do well in all of their activities but had also behaved better than they would have in Cuba.[54]

The attitude of Americans toward newcomers has been, if anything, schizophrenic. On the one hand, the nation's immigrant heritage has been frequently celebrated. On the other, nativism and suspicion have always met newcomers. The paradox was not absent during the years of Cuban immigration. The children who were placed in local communities across the country encountered both support and opposition. Complaints of more being done for Cuban children than for their own were heard from many Americans. There were also reports of resistance by school boards to educating nonresidents when children were not enrolled in Catholic schools.[55] To counteract the impression that the federal government was doing more for Cuban than for American children, Walsh defended the program before a congressional committee.[56] In any case, the children seem to have been more welcomed than resented by the communities of which they became a part.

All their adaptability, however, could not compensate for the children's separation from their families and all that was familiar to them. Their encounter with the strange and unknown had come suddenly and shockingly. In the documentary film *Lost Apple*, the narrator stated, "You can't stay lonely forever."[57] That statement was an acknowledgment by officials that, despite adaptation, the children were still plagued by loneliness. Reports of loneliness from teenage boys suggest that the younger children suffered even more.

A sense of loneliness was evident from the children's emotional dependence on Cuban adults during the separation from their parents. Such evidence was seen in nearly all the letters the children sent to Sara Yaballi, one of the nurses at Matecumbe, when they were sent away from Miami.[58] The boys often referred to Yaballi as "Mother" or "Aunt Sara." Yaballi acknowledged her role as a substitute mother for some boys. Performing acts that were well beyond her responsibilities (such as voluntarily ironing some of the boys' clothes), she won their affection and love.[59] A letter from Pablo, relocated to Helena, Montana, typified the tone of the correspondence: "I received your long-awaited letter a few minutes ago and I am now responding after lunch. Your letters always please me, because I know that although I do not have you by my side, you are always concerned about us and your bountiful heart is always with us; that is the reason we love you so much, as if you were a mother to us; we have you now that our real ones are missing."[60]

Other boys wrote Yaballi in a similar vein, one even offering to send her money when she was unemployed and another gallantly proclaiming that he would give his life for her.[61] Virtually all the boys expressed their gratitude for her tenderness, kindness, and guidance.[62]

Yaballi was the recipient of many Mother's Day cards, as were other substitute Cuban parents. Gina Baena, a worker at St. Raphael's, at Whitehall, and later at the boys' centers on Southwest Eighth Street and Biscayne Boulevard, claimed to have once received sixty-nine Mother's Day gifts from more than one hundred boys. One even sent her a card from Vietnam.[63] Alberto Cuartas, a counselor and houseparent with the Cuban Children's Program from 1962 to 1981, received a Father's Day card from one of those named Roberto: "From one of your sons who in less than five months has learned to appreciate you like a father in this exile; hopefully next year I will not be sending this card to Miami but to a free Cuba, God willing."[64]

The attachments formed between the children and the adults were no doubt based on cultural factors. As children in different cultures are conditioned to receive affection and love in different ways, adult Cubans were more aware of the type of treatment a Cuban child needed in order to feel loved and cared for. Years later, Father Walsh publicly acknowledged the key role that Cuban adults played in the program. His appreciation and admiration for those individuals was evident.[65]

The children's love for the adults was also apparent in their longing to return to the days at "the green hell,"[66] as one boy writing from Lincoln, Nebraska, nostalgically called Matecumbe. Many claimed that, in spite of their discomfort, they missed the friends they had made at the transit centers, both adults and peers.[67]

The children's parents, also suffering from estrangement, found comfort in the Cuban adults who took the children under their wings. Most of the parents' letters to Yaballi spoke to both those issues. Parents thanked her graciously for the love, affection, and guidance she gave their children. They frequently expressed their love for their children and their longing to be reunited with them.[68] One mother wrote, in a typical vein:

> I write you these lines motivated by the good feelings I have for you, as my sons have told me of how kind and loving you are with them. I deeply appreciate your friendliness toward them, whom I love so much and from whom I find myself so far away because of the horrible circumstances that our fatherland, so loved and disgraced, is going through. They have told me that you and I are similar, and that unites them to a ribbon of love; my poor little ones, we have never been separated, but God willing I hope to be with them soon and then I will have the pleasure of embracing them.[69]

Another parent wrote Yaballi, "Yesterday was 14 months since he left, and I was able to speak to him on the telephone. The truth is that I became very nervous and he also appeared to be nervous, as he spoke little. His voice seemed unfamiliar to me. His father became very emotional and could not speak much either."[70]

The children, although lonely and somewhat disoriented, adjusted to their situations with stoic determination and various coping mechanisms. In the end, most children who had been well adjusted in Cuba adjusted to life in exile and to their separation.[71] In one such case, Pedro, a teenager sent to Wilmington, Delaware, after a time at Matecumbe, wrote to Yaballi shortly after his arrival in Delaware in August 1962:

> How I miss your advice, now that we are more alone than ever. . . . It is an emotion that I have never felt. In Miami all we were missing were our parents, and all of you [adult Cubans] were their representatives. We had the Fatherland nearby, which was why we did not miss it so much. Now, well, now I have only one good friend in whom I confide: God. I see the Fatherland more distant than ever and I do not have my parents and I see you battling for the good of those children who one day will take the same road all of us did through this hell.[72]

Pedro's adjustment was stunningly quick. He wrote just over a month later:

> I do not know whether to tell you that I no longer feel so alone or that I have become accustomed. Perhaps it is because of the start of the school year and making new friends; the point is that each day I see the doors more open. Although I also see obstacles in the way, they will be surmounted by faith and sacrifice. To give you an idea of how busy I am, I will tell you what I do now that classes are in session. Every day I wake up at 6:30 a.m. to help the father [priest] give mass (in the house's little chapel). From 8:45 a.m. to 2:45 p.m. [I am] in school. Later I study until 5:30 or 6 p.m., which is dinnertime, and at 7:30 I go back to studying until 9:30 or 10:00 p.m. Saturdays and Sundays we have more free time. Even so, we have to study some on Saturdays and on Sunday night, since they give us a good deal of homework.[73]

Pedro's letters were loaded with typical complaints and coping mechanisms. In the first letter, he demonstrated his emotional attachment to Cuban adults and his disappointment at being sent away from Matecumbe. The second letter described Pedro's adaptation. The underlying theme of the second letter was that he was kept busy, and it was such activities that were the key to his adaptation.

Primarily, Pedro was kept busy with schoolwork. Psychologist Lourdes Rodriguez discovered that academic excellence was a key coping mechanism among Pedro Pan children, who thought that it was important for them to be at the top of their class. In fact, she stated that getting good grades in school was the children's top priority.[74] While the children were motivated by a desire to show themselves worthy to their parents and caretakers, school activities gave them an avenue through which to channel their energies and passions. Virtually all of the letters written to Yaballi gave reports on academic progress. Some spoke of plans for college.[75] Academic excellence meant acquiring English skills, which were of great importance in giving the students greater economic opportunity whether they stayed in the United States or returned to Cuba. Furthermore, proficiency in English would ease the way when their parents arrived to begin lives in exile.[76] The narrator of *The Lost Apple* emphasized that point when he spoke of the importance of studying and the power of education.[77]

In his first letter, Pedro wrote of God as of a close friend; in his time of depression, Pedro turned to his spiritual life. Reverting to faith was a typical reaction. Most boys who wrote to Yaballi spoke of God, sometimes in elaborate terms. One even sent a copy of a prayer.[78]

Some children were instructed by their parents to look out for younger siblings and to keep the family together. That duty was frustrating for many, and some felt powerless to fulfill their parents' wishes. Although program directors made an effort to keep brothers and sisters together, age and sex differences sometimes caused them to become separated in certain types of institutions.[79] Nevertheless, being charged with a major responsibility, such as achieving academic excellence or watching over a younger sibling, gave many children a mission to carry out and helped them cope with their situations. In addition, it gave the younger ones a sense of security and protection.

Keeping the children focused on certain activities helped them endure the pain of estrangement from their homeland, their parents, and, for those sent away from Miami, their culture. That fact was not lost on the program's coordinators, who did their best to engage the children in rewarding activities and to help them avoid idleness at the transit centers, which were under their direct control.

The presence of other Cuban youths in similar circumstances was another positive force in adaptation. Daniel Merida remembered that despite the cliques and the rivalries, there was a sense of togetherness when facing an outside world that often seemed hostile and nativist. The camaraderie that existed, especially among immediate peer groups, was a great source of strength. The children's letters and cards frequently referred to the friends they had left at the transit centers and the comfort they found in the new ones they were making.

Contact with other Cubans also fostered a sense of nationalism. One boy wrote with great passion from Portland, Oregon, "If everyone leaves Miami, who will fight for Cuba? Is it just to send American soldiers? No, Sara, it is our responsibility and [we are the] ones who must sacrifice ourselves."[80] Another boy, missing no opportunity to propagate the Cuban cause, wrote on the back of an envelope he sent: "Wake up America! Stamp out Communism! Pray for Cuba."[81]

Coping Mechanisms

Some children coped with their conflicts by expressing resentment toward their parents. Older children sometimes became frustrated at the delay in reunion with family. Having believed that the separation would last for at most a few months, some became confused and angry when months became years. Some children felt abandoned. They did not understand why their parents had sent them away, particularly children too young to grasp the underlying situation.[82] For some, then, adaptation to a life of separation was tied to resentment, which may have made things easier in the short run. Although not all Pedro Pan children felt antagonistic, many questioned their parents' motives, especially those who experienced long separations. For some, the resentments melted away when they were reunited, but others carried their anger for years.[83]

Yet the most astonishing and impressive characteristic the children displayed was their stoicism. Kathryn Close reported that social workers were impressed with their charges' "emotional strength which has enabled the majority of children to take such a precarious separation from their parents with apparent calmness."[84] She added, "While some of them have been found crying at night by their foster parents, relatively few have been reported as showing symptoms of severe emotional disturbance."[85] Tears in the night may have been more common than Close thought, but it was clear that the children found it important to keep their emotions to themselves or to share them with only a few. Most important, it was vital to hide their difficulties from their parents. Realizing that their families would only feel worse because of the inability to be of help, the children often hid their loneliness and fears when writing letters or speaking to their parents on the telephone.[86] Aurora Candelaria remembered comforting her mother: "We told her, 'Mother we are alright, but please come quickly,' and everyone [was] crying. I mean, that was an experience. . . . We never told her we were at an orphanage, never, because we knew that would have been the end [in her mind]."[87]

Margarita Oteiza remembered, with some admiration, the children's bravery:

Many of the children never told their parents of the very difficult situation they encountered here. They presented—and those were children who I admired for the love they had for their parents—they presented a "No, everything is well, here we are [well]" attitude; and they were not well. They were taken care of and safe but they were not well. There is a big difference. You have to remember that these were children of professionals in Cuba, children who were overpro-tected. It did not matter if they were boys, it did not matter how old they were, they were still mommy's and daddy's children and they got here and suddenly had to grow up overnight. They had to face things overnight they never had to face before.[88]

The Lost Apple included a scene of a Florida City girl who had just received a telephone call from her parents in Cuba. Excitedly running into the public telephone booth, she was followed by a large group of girls. She picked up the receiver, took a deep breath, and began to speak. Her voice was calm and confident at first, but after a time she could not fight back tears. She seemed relieved when the person at the other end was speaking, as it gave her an opportunity to control her emotions and regain her com-posure when it was once again her turn to speak. In an obvious struggle to produce a cheerful voice, she reported that everything was just fine and that she was crying from joy. The group of girls who followed her sur-rounded the telephone booth and quietly looked in through its glass walls. The expressions on their faces evoked a feeling of vicarious happiness. They seemed to want to be as close as possible to the friend who was speaking to her parents, as if some of its effect would overflow to them.[89]

Nearly all the children interviewed agreed that hearing from parents was an important event. When Yaballi's boys received word from home, they would tell her all the news—often little more than trivial family happenings. Nevertheless, even such details gave them pleasure.[90] The telephone calls were more exciting than letters because their parents' voices came alive for them. Yaballi called telephone calls the "greatest moments" for the children.[91]

Repression Eventually Takes Its Toll

The Pedro Pan children's stoicism nevertheless came with a price many had to pay years later. Many coping mechanisms provided a vehicle for denial, which was perhaps a necessary means of psychological survival when they were separated from their parents. Lourdes Rodriguez stated that, having been indoctrinated by their parents to act grown-up in isolation, many children, who also focused intently on responsibilities and tried to protect parents by concealing their distress, in fact repressed the powerful emotions that would be expected in their circumstances. In other words, many children, instead of surmounting their emotional difficulties, only forestalled their emergence. Rodriguez referred to this as a "delay-grief process," a normal phenomenon that exists within a great variety of contexts.

The emotions that Lourdes Rodriguez and her subjects had repressed emerged years later, when they were adults. Never having forgotten the details of their experience as children, as adults they began suffering irrational panics, fears, and anxieties on specific occasions. Usually, the symptoms resulted from a subconscious connection between the experience as a child refugee and an unassociated event in adulthood that triggered the reactions. For instance, when Rodriguez was preparing for a trip to Europe before writing her doctoral dissertation in 1982, she was struck by severe abdominal pains and the irrational fear that she was going to die while abroad. Although she ultimately went to Europe, her fears and anxieties did not subside. Upon her return, she experienced anxiety and panic attacks every time she left Boston, usually when she had traveled only a few miles from her home. Rodriguez went into therapy and was told her condition had to do with her separation from her parents as a child. Although at first she did not believe that the years-earlier experience had anything to do with her present condition, Rodriguez eventually came to accept that, despite a successful adulthood, she had repressed the feelings she should have experienced as a child and must thus deal with them as an adult. The trip to Europe, which triggered the association, unleashed a barrage of repressed childhood emotions.

The histories of Rodriguez's subjects mirrored that of the researcher. In many cases, the emotional association emerged at a time when the subject was traveling or moving from one residence to another. Like Rodriguez, none drew an immediate connection with the experience of being a child refugee and came to terms with the condition only after therapy or after sharing feelings with someone. Rodriguez also noted that in some cases the emotional association came when a person's child reached the age at which that person had been sent away from Cuba.[92]

Nine

Reunited at Last:
A Dream Come True or a
Shock of Recognition?

The reunion of parents and children was among the most poignant and the most difficult parts of the Pedro Pan and Cuban Children's Program experience. Many children likened it to a dream come true. Others found their parents strange and different. Coupled with the resentment some children harbored, unfamiliarity furthered their animosity and made readjustment more strenuous. Despite the conflicting emotions, the moment a child saw his parents for the first time in months or years was usually one of great joy.

The reunions came at various junctures. Some children were reunited within a few days or months because their parents were able to leave Cuba prior to the Cuban missile crisis. Some parents made it to the United States by fleeing to third countries, where they applied for U.S. visas. For a large number, reunification occurred during 1965 or soon thereafter.

In late September 1965, the Cuban government announced that any Cuban with relatives in the United States was free to go there after October 10. Less than a week later, President Lyndon B. Johnson signed a new immigration bill and announced that those seeking refuge in the United States would find it. In early October, the Cuban government designated the port of Camarioca as the point of embarkation. The massive exodus that ensued resulted in a number of deaths at sea, as desperate relatives often sailed from Cuba in unseaworthy craft. Zeal to retrieve family members overcame caution. Within a few weeks the chaos resulted in an acknowledgment by the Cuban and U.S. governments of the need for a more orderly and less precarious system to facilitate the exodus.

In November the two governments signed a memorandum of understanding that provided for the systematic, orderly airlift of Cubans who wished to emigrate to the United States. Cubans with relatives in the United States, especially unmarried children under twenty-one and siblings, were to be given priority on the Freedom Flights, as they were called. Most of the Operation Pedro Pan children still under the care of the Cuban Children's Program were reunited with their parents during the earliest stages of the Freedom Flights.

Because relocating Cubans outside Miami was still a popular notion, parents were encouraged to settle wherever their children had been sent. Many complied and moved to those areas, at least temporarily. Because the heavy influx of minors had ended in 1962, after the Cuban missile crisis, the policy of relocating children to other parts of the country had been discontinued, and unplaced children stayed in Miami—the boys at the Opa-Locka center, the Eighth Street center, or Biscayne Boulevard, and the girls at Florida City or the home on U.S. Highway 1. Many who had been discharged before 1965 were also in Miami when the Freedom Flights started.

The moment when a child saw his or her parents for the first time after their separation was poignant and compelling, as related by those who cared for boys in Miami. Their experiences were probably similar to those of the other children. Program administrators in Miami knew a few days beforehand the date when a particular child's parents would be arriving. Alberto Cuartas was in charge of delivering the good news to the boys and taking them to the airport to greet their estranged parents. Each morning, he received the list of those who were to arrive on that afternoon's flights. The children learned that news that morning only at the last minute, so as to keep their anxiety to a minimum, as most reacted strongly when informed. While awaiting their trip to the airport, they became nervous and a number vomited, fainted, or were struck with diarrhea. Most would not eat lunch. None went to school. All put on their best clothes.[1]

Cuartas witnessed dramatic moments of reunion. He remembered, "Many parents did not recognize their children. The children recognized them immediately. They would say, 'Look, there they are, there they are,' then they would break into a run and then stand before them and many parents would look and look at them until they finally recognized them. It was fantastic. I would take ill, because I am very emotional. . . . Every day it was tears, embraces, tears."[2]

Fortunately, most Pedro Pan children were reunited with their parents. Exceptions were few. For many, the lives that followed immediately thereafter were difficult, both financially and emotionally. There were children who believed that their parents did not love them because they had sent them away.[3] Such families needed a time of healing. For others, a seemingly unbreachable cultural rift had developed during their separation.[4] Some had grown accustomed to a different type of home environment and had difficulty reaccepting their parents' authority.[5] Still, families ultimately adapted well to their new situation. Children commonly accepted leadership roles in the family after reunification because of their parents' ignorance about life in the United States and their inability to speak English.[6]

Whatever the specific situation, family life was never the same. It may not have been worse than in Cuba, but the years of separation and their subsequent lives as exiles were, for all families, a new and challenging prospect. Life in the United States had begun for them, and the United States was in possession of a new generation of Americans.

Ten

An Evaluation:
How Successful Was the Rescue Operation?

In evaluating Operation Pedro Pan and the Cuban Children's Program, this book finds that Pedro Pan was clearly successful in responding to Cuban parents' needs and wishes. The Cuban underground and Father Walsh helped 14,048 children leave Cuba for the United States. The Cuban Children's Program was equally successful. In spite of the overall sense of loneliness and the occasional claims of abuse, the children were well taken care of, especially considering the circumstances and pressures under which the program operated.

Were the United States government and the Catholic Church justified in providing an outlet for children whose parents were panic-stricken? Walsh stated that he and others were not oblivious to that question and that the organizers constantly asked themselves whether they were doing the right thing. In his view they were, and in the end the parents made the decisions.[1] Is Walsh's view valid? To have denied Cuban parents the opportunity to send their children to what they believed represented safety would have been a grave error, like that of the United States in sending boatloads of Jews back to Nazi Germany in the late 1930s. This study concludes that Walsh acted correctly. The United States, moreover, lived up to its historic image of being a sanctuary for the oppressed. It also went a step beyond that image by becoming an active participant, a player.

Many have criticized the program because many children suffered. Such criticisms, although valid to some extent, fail to consider the alternative. Whether or not Castro would have sent the children to the USSR or into the Cuban countryside for indoctrination, it was clear that parental control over children's lives was going to be transferred largely to the state. When it came time for the decision either to submit to the state—representing a system that the parents found repugnant—or to send the children to safety in the United States, where political and religious freedom were assured, the Cuban parents opted for the latter. It was the parents and not the state that made the decision. Even if the children could not return to Cuba, the parents who sent them to the United States could at least look forward to joining them there and reassuming their roles as parents. As far as they could see, that resumption of roles would not have occurred in Cuba.

Other criticisms of the Cuban Children's Program smack strongly of political ideology. Grupo Areito, a group of Cubans in the United States who are sympathetic to the Castro regime, includes some former Pedro Pan children who have stated, as recounted by Joan Didion, that the distinction between being sent to camps in Russia and camps in the United States was insignificant for the young refugees.[2] I read a quotation from Didion's *Miami* expressing this viewpoint to a group of people interviewed for this book and asked whether they agreed with the Areito members. The interviewees included ten people who had been Pedro Pan children and several who had been involved in the programs as adults. Upon hearing the quotation, all of them looked puzzled. Some found it so incomprehensible that they asked me to read it again. Not one person agreed with this viewpoint, and most were shocked by it. None of the many letters I studied support the position of the Areito members, who have declared that the exodus of the Cuban youngsters was used merely as a propaganda ploy.[3] In fact, those involved with Operation Pedro Pan and the Cuban Children's Program did everything possible to keep their work low-profile. When Walsh issued a press release in 1962 about the rescues, it came only after the *Cleveland Plain Dealer* threatened to run a story about them.

Those who were the children of Operation Pedro Pan have been credited, as adults, with a certain inner strength, which is attributed to their having to endure such a trauma at a young age. Many have pointed to their successful careers as evidence. By the 1990s their ranks included renowned recording artists, lawyers, physicians, college professors, high-ranking clergy, corporate leaders, and many other professionals. Their individual successes or failures in the years after Operation Pedro Pan and the Cuban Children's Program have yet to be explored. On the basis of the accessible information, it would be a timely and enlightening work.

Appendix

Operation Pedro Pan Group, Inc.

Operation Pedro Pan Group, Inc., was founded by former Pedro Pan children in June 1991, following the death of George Guarch. The group received the blessing of Monsignor Bryan O. Walsh and recognition from the Archdiocese of Miami. It was granted nonprofit organization status from the federal government and an official service mark from the U.S. Department of Commerce.[1]

The Pedro Pan Group is dedicated to "help[ing] today's dependent children and those who continue to arrive unaccompanied to these shores."[2] Its immediate goal is the creation of a Children's Village as a prototype child-care facility where children live in a homelike atmosphere and siblings stay together.[3]

Operation Pedro Pan Group had become highly visible in Dade County by the mid-1990s. The organization has received frequent press coverage for both its charitable activities and its social events. Pedro Pans who have become celebrities in the music world and elsewhere are present at such events.

Among those who enjoy alumni status are Lisette Alvarez, Willy Chirino, Carlos Oliva, and Marisela Verena. Chirino and Verena, who have sung moving songs about their experience as refugees, were joined by Alvarez and Oliva in producing an album. The proceeds from album sales go to Catholic Family Services' Refugee Resettlement Program. The songs on the album, anchored in the singers' experiences as child refugees, were popular in Cuba or the United States at the time they sought refuge. The songs include "The Twist," "Hit the Road Jack," "Breaking Up Is Hard to Do," and "The Lion Sleeps Tonight," and a number of Spanish-language songs.[4]

The album also features Lizbet Martinez's violin rendition of the Cuban and United States national anthems. She was one of the many Cuban children in a state of limbo at the U.S. Naval Base at Guantanamo, Cuba, awaiting entry into the United States after President Bill Clinton shut the door on Cuban refugees in August 1994. The beauty of her contribution demonstrates not only a high level of musical talent but also great depth of feeling.[5]

The album cover depicts the four Pedro Pan artists looking from the windows of a school bus driven by Monsignor Walsh. The cover was designed by eight-year-old Daniel Bussot, who left Cuba for the United States on a raft in 1994. When the raft encountered rough seas, his parents gave Daniel the only available lifejacket, and the two perished in the Florida Straits.[6]

The most interesting song on the album is a modified version of the "Conga del Campamento" (Camp Conga), a song composed by the Pedro Pan children while at the transit centers. The song's lyrics are sung in Spanish to the rhythmic clapping of a conga beat and read in their original form:

We are Cubans—so listen to us well—
Who came in refuge and blame it on Fidel.
And to the Americans we want to tell,
That we are like brothers and get along well.
And to the Communists we want to say,
That from lovely little Cuba you must go away.
And to the Virgin of Charity we want to say,
That from lovely little Cuba you must take them away.[7]

Notes

One. The Panic Begins

1. Fagen, Brody, and O'Leary, *Cubans in Exile*, 101.
2. Walsh, "Cuban Refugee Children," 383–84.
3. Walsh, March 21, 1992, speech.
4. Fagen, Brody, and O'Leary, *Cubans in Exile*, 83.
5. H. Thomas, *The Cuban Revolution*, 502.
6. Baker interview, June 4, 1994.
7. Ponte interview, June 2, 1994.
8. Nelson, *Cuba: The Measure of a Revolution*, 136.
9. Ibid., 137, 138.
10. H. Thomas, *The Cuban Revolution*, 561, 562.
11. *Time*, "And Now the Children?" 41; Nelson, *Cuba: The Measure of a Revolution*, 148.
12. *Time*, "And Now the Children?" 41.
13. Clark interview, May 31, 1994.
14. Nelson, *Cuba: The Measure of a Revolution*, 152.
15. Clark, March 21, 1992, speech.
16. Walsh, March 21, 1992, speech.

Two. Operation Pedro Pan

1. *Miami Herald*, May 24, 1994.
2. Oettinger and Thomas, *Cuba's Children in Exile*, 1.
3. Walsh, "Cuban Refugee Children," 387.
4. Oettinger and Thomas, *Cuba's Children in Exile*, foreword.
5. McNally, *Catholicism*, 144.
6. Walsh, "Cuban Refugee Children," 387.

7. Ibid., 388.

8. Ibid.

9. Ibid.

10. Voorhees, interim report, cited in Walsh, "Cuban Refugee Children," 389.

11. Baker interview, June 4, 1994.

12. Ibid.

13. Walsh, "Cuban Refugee Children," 390.

14. Baker interview, June 4, 1994.

15. Ibid.

16. Ibid.

17. Walsh, "Cuban Refugee Children," 391.

18. Ibid., 394.

19. Walsh, "Cuban Refugee Children," 395.

20. Ibid.

21. Ibid., 396.

22. Walsh interview, May 24, 1994.

23. Ibid.

24. Baker interview, June 4, 1994.

Three. International Intrigue

1. Baker interview, June 4, 1994; Walsh, "Cuban Refugee Children," 399.

2. Walsh, "Cuban Refugee Children," 400; Walsh interview, May 24, 1994.

3. Walsh, "Cuban Refugee Children," 400.

4. Ibid., 401.

5. Cortes, *Cuban Refugee Programs*, 206, citing statement of Robert F. Hale, director, Visa Office, December 13, 1961.

6. Walsh, "Cuban Refugee Children," 401.

7. Ibid.

8. Ibid., 402.

9. Cortes, *Cuban Refugee Programs*, 206, citing Hale, Visa Office, December 13, 1961.

10. Close, "Cuban Children Away From Home," 6.

11. J. F. Thomas, "Cuban Refugee Program," 6.

12. Mitchell, "The Cuban Refugee Program," 4.

13. J. F. Thomas, "Cuban Refugee Program," 6; Cortes, *Cuban Refugee Programs*, 206, citing Hale, Visa Office, December 13, 1961.

14. Walsh, telephone conversation, May 22, 1995.

15. Walsh, "Cuban Refugee Children," 400–402.

16. Ibid., 406.

17. Walsh, March 21, 1992, speech.

18. Baker interview, June 4, 1994.

19. Walsh, telephone conversation, October 21, 1994.

20. Ibid.

21. "The Continuing Need," 257–59, testimony of Roger Jones, deputy under-secretary for administration.

22. Masud-Piloto, *With Open Arms*, 52.

23. Walsh, March 21, 1992, speech.

Four. Behind the Iron Curtain

1. Walsh interview, May 24, 1994.

2. Walsh, "Cuban Refugee Children," 383.

3. Reed, "Flight of Fear," 7, 8.

4. L. Grau interview, May 30, 1994; R. Grau Alsina interview, May 31, 1994; O'Farrill interview, June 3, 1994.

5. L. Grau interview, May 30, 1994; O'Farrill interview, June 3, 1994.

6. McNally, *Catholicism*, 148.

7. Fuentes interview, June 4, 1994.

8. Ibid.

9. Walsh interview, May 24, 1994.

10. Ibid.

11. Ibid.

12. "Free Transportation," 238.

13. Baker interview, June 4, 1994.

14. Solana interview, September 14, 1994.

15. Fuentes interview, June 4, 1994.

16. O'Farrill interview, June 3, 1994.

17. Baker interview, June 4, 1994.

18. Operation Pedro Pan Group, November 27, 1993.

19. Ibid.; Vilano-Chovel interview, May 24, 1994.

20. Walsh, "Cuban Refugee Children," 391.

21. Baker interview, June 4, 1994.

22. Walsh interview, May 24, 1994; Vilano-Chovel interview, May 24, 1994; de la Torriente interview, May 30, 1994.

23. De la Torriente interview, May 30, 1994.

24. Walsh interview, May 24, 1994.

25. De la Torriente interview, May 30, 1994.

26. O'Farrill interview, June 3, 1994.

27. *Times* (London), November 27, 1992.

28. L. Grau interview, May 30, 1994.

29. Ibid.

30. L. Grau interview, May 30, 1994; R. Grau Alsina interview, May 31, 1994.

31. L. Grau interview, May 30, 1994.

32. Ibid.

33. Ibid.

34. R. Grau Alsina interview, May 31, 1994.

35. Del Toro interview, May 31, 1994.

36. Ibid.

37. Ibid.

38. De la Torriente interview, May 30, 1994.

39. O'Farrill interview, June 3, 1994; Operation Pedro Pan Group, November 27, 1993.

Five. Helping Cubans Escape Tyranny

1. Mitchell, "The Cuban Refugee Program," 3.

2. J. F. Thomas, "Cuban Refugee Program," 1, 2.

3. Mitchell, "The Cuban Refugee Program," 4.

4. J. F. Thomas, "Cuban Refugees in U.S.," 48; J. Thomas, "Cuban Refugee Program," 5.

5. Oettinger and Thomas, *Cuba's Children in Exile*, 12.

6. J. F. Thomas, "Cuban Refugee Program," 4.

7. Mitchell, "The Cuban Refugee Program," 4.

8. J. F. Thomas, "Cuban Refugee Program," 4.

9. Walsh, "Cuban Refugee Children," 386.

10. *Miami Herald*, September 5, 1997.

11. J. F. Thomas, "Cuban Refugee Program," 6.

12. J. F. Thomas, "Cuban Refugees in U.S.," 48.

13. J. F. Thomas, "Cuban Refugee Program," 5, 6.

14. J. F. Thomas, "U.S.A. as Country of First," 5.

15. Walsh, "Cuban Refugee Children," 411, 412.

16. Oettinger and Thomas, *Cuba's Children in Exile*, 3; Close, "Cuban Children Away from Home," 4; Oettinger, "Services to Unaccompanied Cuban Children," 379.

17. Ressler, Boothby, and Steinbock, *Unaccompanied Children*, 54.

18. Walsh, telephone conversation, September 1, 1994.

19. Oettinger and Thomas, *Cuba's Children in Exile*, 4.

20. Ressler, Boothby, and Steinbock, *Unaccompanied Children*, 53; Oettinger and Thomas, *Cuba's Children in Exile*, 4.

21. Close, "Cuban Children Away from Home," 9; Oettinger, "Services to Unaccompanied Cuban Children," 381; Oettinger and Thomas, *Cuba's Children in Exile*, 4.

22. Cortes, *Cuban Refugee Programs*, 260, citing statement of James P. Rice, ex-

ecutive director, United HIAS, December 13, 1961; McNally, *Catholicism*, 144.

23. Oettinger, "Services to Unaccompanied Cuban Children, 381; Close, "Cuban Children Away from Home," 9, 10.

24. Ressler, Boothby, and Steinbock, *Unaccompanied Children*, 53.

25. Walsh interview, May 24, 1994.

26. Ibid.

Six. The Cuban Children's Program

1. *Miami Herald*, October 2, 1962.

2. Cortes, *Cuban Refugee Programs*, 66, citing statement of Arthur Rochiman, director, Miami Jewish Federation, December 7, 1961.

3. Ibid., 260, citing statement of Rice, United HIAS, December 13, 1961.

4. Ibid., 167, citing statement of Rochiman, Miami Jewish Federation, December 7, 1961.

5. Oettinger and Thomas, *Cuba's Children in Exile*, 6; Close, "Cuban Children Away From Home," 5.

6. *Miami Herald*.

7. Walsh, telephone conversation, September 1, 1994.

8. Close, "Cuban Children Away From Home," 5.

9. Oettinger and Thomas, *Cuba's Children in Exile*, 6; Close, "Cuban Children Away From Home," 5.

10. Close, "Cuban Children Away From Home," 5, 6.

11. Walsh, telephone conversation, September 1, 1994.

12. Walsh, March 21, 1992, speech.

13. Vilano-Chovel, telephone conversation, October 11, 1997.

14. Walsh, March 21, 1992, speech.

15. Ibid.

16. First Research Corporation, "Cost Analysis," 6.

17. Walsh, "Cuban Refugee Children," 393.

18. Walsh, March 21, 1992, speech.

19. Cuartas interview, June 3, 1994.

20. Walsh, "Cuban Refugee Children," 399, 408.

21. Ramudo interview, June 1, 1994.

22. Adessa, "Refugee Cuban Children," 84.

23. Ibid., 86.

24. Cuartas interview, June 3, 1994; Adessa, "Refugee Cuban Children," 84.

25. Cuartas interview, June 3, 1994.

26. Walsh, March 21, 1992, speech.

27. Close, "Cuban Children Away From Home," 10; Walsh, "Cuban Refugee Children," 406.

28. Adessa, "Refugee Cuban Children," 88.

29. Cuartas interview, June 3, 1994.

30. Adessa, "Refugee Cuban Children," 88, 90; Cuartas interview, June 3, 1994; Oteiza interview, June 5, 1994; Merida interview, November 26, 1994; *New York Times*, May 27, 1962.

31. Ling interview, June 2, 1994.

32. Adessa, "Refugee Cuban Children," 90, 91.

33. Cuartas File, Operation Pedro Pan Collection.

34. Cuartas interview, June 3, 1994.

35. Walsh, March 21, 1992, speech.

36. Adessa, "Refugee Cuban Children," 91, 94; Cuartas interview, June 3, 1994.

37. Cuartas interview, June 3, 1994; Adessa, "Refugee Cuban Children," 94.

38. Cuartas interview, June 3, 1994.

39. Adessa, "Refugee Cuban Children," 99, 100.

40. Baena interview, May 26, 1994; Cuartas interview, June 3, 1994; Garcia interview, May 26, 1994; Ramudo interview, June 1, 1994; Adessa, "Refugee Cuban Children," 95.

41. Adessa, "Refugee Cuban Children," 96; Cuartas interview, June 3, 1994.

42. Cuartas interview, June 3, 1994.

43. Adessa, "Cuban Refugee Children," 86.

44. Walsh, telephone conversation, May 22, 1995.

45. Cuartas interview, June 3, 1994.

46. Walsh, telephone conversation, May 22, 1995.

47. Walsh, March 21, 1992, speech.

48. Walsh, "Cuban Refugee Children," 379, 412.

49. Adessa, "Refugee Cuban Children," 105, 111.

50. Walsh, "Cuban Refugee Children," 409.

51. Adessa, "Refugee Cuban Children," 104.

52. Walsh, "Cuban Refugee Children," 413.

53. Adessa, "Refugee Cuban Children," 112.

54. *Christian Century*, "Refugee Cuban Children Need Homes," 417.

55. Walsh, March 21, 1992, speech; Adessa, "Refugee Cuban Children," 109; Merida interview, November 26, 1994.

56. McNally, *Catholicism*, 149.

57. Oteiza interview, June 5, 1994.

58. Adessa, "Refugee Cuban Children," 114.

59. Ibid., 117.

60. Oteiza interview, June 5, 1994.

61. Cuartas interview, June 3, 1994; Oteiza interview, June 5, 1994.

62. Walsh, March 21, 1992, speech.

63. Close, "Cuban Children Away From Home," 8, 9.

Seven. A Watershed Experience

1. Close, "Cuban Children Away From Home," 6, 7; First Research Corporation, "Cost Analysis," 4; Oettinger and Thomas, *Cuba's Children in Exile*, 7.
2. Close, "Cuban Children Away From Home," 6, 7; Oettinger and Thomas, *Cuba's Children in Exile*, 7.
3. Anonymous, interview, June 3, 1994.
4. Carrera interview, May 25, 1994.
5. *St. Petersburg Times*, November 4, 1990.
6. Merida interview, November 26, 1994.
7. Ibid.
8. Candelaria interview, June 1, 1994.
9. Ponte interview, June 2, 1994.
10. Merida interview, November 26, 1994.
11. Anonymous, interview, June 3, 1994.
12. Vilano-Chovel interview, May 24, 1994.
13. Rodriguez, March 21, 1992, speech.
14. Baker interview, June 4, 1994; Oteiza interview, June 5, 1994; Walsh, "Cuban Refugee Children," 395.
15. Oteiza interview, June 5, 1994.
16. *New York Times*, May 27, 1962.
17. Vilano-Chovel interview, May 24, 1994.
18. *New York Times*, May 27, 1962.
19. Vilano-Chovel interview, May 24, 1994.
20. Candelaria interview, June 1, 1994.
21. Ling interview, June 2, 1994.
22. Hubbel, "Operacion Pedro Pan," 30–2.
23. Merida interview, November 26, 1994.
24. Oteiza interview, June 5, 1994.
25. Susskin, *The Lost Apple* (film).

Eight. Toward a Resolution

1. Yaballi files, Operation Pedro Pan Collection.
2. Close, "Cuban Children Away From Home," 6.
3. Vilano-Chovel interview, May 24, 1994.
4. Susskin, *The Lost Apple* (film).
5. Ramudo interview, June 1, 1994.
6. Anonymous interview, June 3, 1994.
7. Ling interview, June 2, 1994.

8. Merida interview, November 26, 1994.

9. Oteiza interview, June 5, 1994.

10. Baena interview, May 24, 1994.

11. Walsh, March 21, 1992, speech.

12. Adessa, "Refugee Cuban Children," 95.

13. Ramudo interview, June 1, 1994.

14. Garcia interview, May 26, 1994.

15. Ibid.

16. Hubbel, "Operacion Pedro Pan," 32.

17. Ibid.

18. Garcia interview, May 26, 1994.

19. *Voice*, 1968.

20. Vilano-Chovel interview, November 26, 1994.

21. Walsh, "Cuban Refugee Children," 412.

22. Close, "Cuban Children Away From Home," 8.

23. Yaballi files, Operation Pedro Pan Collection.

24. Adessa, "Refugee Cuban Children," 111.

25. Anonymous interview, June 3, 1994.

26. Walsh, March 21, 1992, speech.

27. Borrego interview, May 23, 1994.

28. Candelaria interview, June 1, 1994.

29. Oettinger and Thomas, *Cuba's Children in Exile*, 7; Ressler, Boothby, and Steinbock, *Unaccompanied Children*, 54; Baena interview, May 24, 1994.

30. Carrera interview, May 25, 1994.

31. Yaballi files, Operation Pedro Pan Collection.

32. Ibid.

33. Merida interview, November 26, 1994.

34. Yaballi files, Operation Pedro Pan Collection.

35. Oettinger and Thomas, *Cuba's Children in Exile*, 7.

36. Yaballi files, Operation Pedro Pan Files.

37. Oettinger and Thomas, *Cuba's Children in Exile*, 9; Close, "Cuban Children Away From Home," 9.

38. Close, "Cuban Children Away From Home," 8.

39. Vilano-Chovel interview, May 24, 1994; Candelaria interview, June 1, 1994; Borrego interview, May 23, 1994.

40. Vilano-Chovel interview, May 24, 1994.

41. Ibid.

42. Carrera interview, May 25, 1994; Merida interview, November 26, 1994.

43. Yaballi files, Operation Pedro Pan Collection.

44. Ibid.

45. Ibid.

46. Carrera interview, May 25, 1994.

47. Close, "Cuban Children Away From Home," 6.

48. Oettinger and Thomas, *Cuba's Children in Exile*, 8.

49. Ibid.

50. Ressler, Boothby, and Steinbock, *Unaccompanied Children*, 53; Oettinger and Thomas, *Cuba's Children in Exile*, 8.

51. Close, "Cuban Children Away From Home," 3.

52. Oettinger and Thomas, *Cuba's Children in Exile*, 7–9.

53. Ibid., 9.

54. Candelaria interview, June 1, 1994; Carrera interview, May 25, 1994; Ramudo interview, June 1, 1994.

55. Close, "Cuban Children Away From Home," 8.

56. Cortes, *Cuban Refugee Programs*, 230, citing statement of Bryan O. Walsh, director, Catholic Welfare Bureau, December 13, 1961.

57. Susskin, *The Lost Apple* (film).

58. Yaballi files, Operation Pedro Pan Collection.

59. Yaballi interview, June 2, 1994.

60. Yaballi files, Operation Pedro Pan Collection.

61. Ibid.

62. Ibid.

63. Baena interview, May 24, 1994.

64. Cuartas files, Operation Pedro Pan Collection.

65. Walsh, March 21, 1992, speech.

66. Yaballi files, Operation Pedro Pan Collection.

67. Yaballi files, Operation Pedro Pan Collection; Cuartas files, Operation Pedro Pan Collection.

68. Yaballi files, Operation Pedro Pan Collection.

69. Ibid.

70. Ibid.

71. Oettinger and Thomas, *Cuba's Children in Exile*, 8.

72. Yaballi files, Operation Pedro Pan Collection.

73. Ibid.

74. Rodriguez, March 21, 1992, speech.

75. Yaballi files, Operation Pedro Pan Collection.

76. Close, "Cuban Children Away From Home," 6; Ressler, Boothby, and Steinbock, *Unaccompanied Children*, 53.

77. Susskin, *The Lost Apple* (film).

78. Yaballi files, Operation Pedro Pan Collection.
79. Rodriguez, March 21, 1992, speech; anonymous, interview, June 3, 1994; Ling interview, June 2, 1994.
80. Yaballi files, Operation Pedro Pan Collection.
81. Ibid.
82. Oettinger and Thomas, *Cuba's Children in Exile*, 8.
83. Ponte interview, June 2, 1994; Anonymous interview, June 3, 1994; Baena interview, June 4, 1994.
84. Close, "Cuban Children Away From Home," 7.
85. Ibid.
86. Rodriguez, March 21, 1992, speech.
87. Candelaria interview, June 1, 1994.
88. Oteiza interview, June 5, 1994.
89. Susskin, *The Lost Apple* (film).
90. Yaballi files, Operation Pedro Pan Collection.
91. Yaballi interview, June 2, 1994.
92. Rodriguez, March 21, 1992, speech.

Nine. Reunited at Last

1. Cuartas interview, June 3, 1994.
2. Ibid.
3. Yaballi interview, June 2, 1994.
4. Cuartas interview, June 3, 1994.
5. Baena interview, May 24, 1994.
6. Vilano-Chovel interview, May 24, 1994; Merida interview, November 26, 1994; Oettinger and Thomas, *Cuba's Children in Exile*, 6.

Ten. An Evaluation

1. Walsh, March 21, 1992, speech.
2. Didion, *Miami*, 125.
3. Didion, *Miami*, citing Grupo Areito's *Contra Viento y Marea*.

Appendix. Operation Pedro Pan Group, Inc.

1. Vilano-Chovel interview, May 24, 1994.
2. Vilano-Chovel interview, May 24, 1994; Operation Pedro Pan Group, November 27, 1993.
3. Vilano-Chovel interview, May 21, 1994.
4. *Miami Herald*, December 4, 1994.
5. Ibid.
6. Ibid.
7. Susskin, *The Lost Apple* (film).

Bibliography

Primary Sources

Interviews by author (tape recordings)

Anonymous participant in Operation Pedro Pan, Miami, June 3, 1994.
Baena, Gina (employee, Catholic Welfare Bureau), Miami, May 24, 1994.
Baker, James, Ormond Beach, Florida, June 4, 1994.
Borrego, Lourdes (participant, OPP), Miami, May 23, 1994.
Candelaria, Aurora (participant, OPP), Miami, June 1, 1994.
Carrera, Maria Teresa (participant, OPP), Miami, May 25, 1994.
Clark, Juan (Department of Sociology, Miami Dade Community College), Miami, May 31, 1994.
Cuartas, Alberto (employee, Catholic Welfare Bureau), Miami, June 3, 1994.
De la Torriente, Elena (Cuban underground operative), Miami, May 30, 1994.
Del Toro, Sara (Cuban underground operative), Miami, May 31, 1994.
Fuentes, Margarita (employee, KLM Airlines), Fort Lauderdale, June 4, 1994.
Garcia, Alfonso (participant, OPP), Coral Gables, May 26, 1994.
Grau, Leopoldina (Cuban underground operative), Miami, May 30, 1994.
Grau Alsina, Ramon (Cuban underground operative), Miami, May 31, 1994.
Izquierdo, Francisco, Miami, June 2, 1994.
Ling, Martin (participant, OPP), Miami, June 2, 1994.
Merida, Daniel (participant, OPP), Middletown, Connecticut, November 26, 1994.
O'Farrill, Albertina (Cuban underground operative), Coral Gables, June 3, 1994.
Oteiza, Margarita (Cuban underground operative, 1960–61; employee, Catholic Welfare Bureau, 1961–62), Miami, June 5, 1994.
Ponte, Teresa (participant, OPP), Miami, June 2, 1994.
Ramudo, Luis (participant, OPP), Miami, June 1, 1994.
Solana, Elena (Cuban refugee), Middletown, Connecticut, September 14, 1994.

Vilano-Chovel, Elisa (participant, OPP), Miami, May 24, 1994.
Walsh, Bryan, Miami, May 24, 1994.
Yaballi, Sara (employee, Catholic Welfare Bureau), Miami, June 2, 1994.

Personal Communications

Vilano-Chovel, Elisa. Telephone conversation with author, October 11, 1997.
Walsh, Bryan O. Telephone conversations with author, September 1, 10, October 21, 1994, May 22, 1995.

Archives

Pedro Pan Collection. Special Collections. Otto G. Richter Library, University of Miami.

Secondary Sources

Government Hearings

Department of State. "The Continuing Need to Aid Refugees and Escapees." *Bulletin* 45 (August 1961):257–59, citing testimony of R. Jones, deputy undersecretary for administration, before Senate Subcommittee on Refugees and Escapees of the Senate Committee of the Judiciary during hearings on *Cuban Refugee Problems*, 87th Cong., 1st sess., July 12, 1961.
U.S. Senate Committee of the Judiciary. *Cuban Refugee Problems: Hearings before the Subcommittee to Investigate Problems Connected to Refugees and Escapees.* 87th Cong., 1st sess., December 1961, and 2d sess., December 1962. In Carlos Cortes, *Cuban Refugee Programs.* New York: Arno Press, 1980.

Newspapers

Diario de las Americas. Miami. 1986, 1990.
El Nuevo Herald. Miami. 1990, 1994.
La Voz. Miami. 1986.
Miami Herald. 1978, 1990, 1992–94, 1997.
New York Times. 1961–62.
St. Petersburg (Florida) Times. 1990.
Times (London). 1992.
Voice. Miami. 1968.

Films

Susskin, D., executive producer. *The Lost Apple.* U.S. Information Agency, 1962.

Books

Bonsal, Philip W. *Cuba, Castro, and the United States.* Pittsburgh: University of Pittsburgh Press, 1971.

Boswell, Thomas D., and James R. Curtis. *The Cuban American Experience: Culture, Images, and Perspectives.* Totowa, N.J.: Rowman and Allanheld Publishers, 1983.

Cortes, Carlos. *Cuban Refugee Programs.* New York: Arno Press, 1980.

Diaz, Jesus. *De la patria y el exilio* (Of the fatherland and exile). Havana: Union de Escritores y Artistas de Cuba, 1979.

Didion, Joan. *Miami.* New York: Pocket Books, 1987.

Fagen, Richard R., Richard A. Brody, and Thomas J. O'Leary. *Cubans in Exile: Disaffection and the Revolution.* Stanford: Stanford University Press, 1968.

Grupo Areito. *Contra Viento y Marea.* Havana: Casa de las Americas, 1978.

Jorge, Antonio, and Raul Moncarz. "The Quantitatively Different and Massive Nature of the Cuban Outflow after Castro's Revolution." In *Cuban Exiles in Florida: Their Presence and Contribution,* ed. Antonio Jorge, Jaime Suchlicki, and Antonio Leyva de Varona, 178–90. Miami: University of Miami North-South Center Publications for the Research Institute for Cuban Studies, 1991.

Langley, Lester D. *The U.S., Cuba, and the Cold War: American Failure or Communist Conspiracy?* Lexington: University Press of Kentucky, 1983.

Llanes, Jose. *Cuban Americans: Masters of Survival.* Cambridge, Mass.: Abt Books, 1982.

MacCorkle, Lyn. *Cubans in the United States: A Bibliography for Research in the Social and Behavioral Sciences, 1960–1983.* Westport, Conn.: Greenwood Press, 1984.

Masud-Piloto, Felix Roberto. *With Open Arms: Cuban Migration to the United States, 1959–1980.* Totowa, N.J.: Rowman and Littlefield Press, 1988.

McNally, Michael. *Catholicism in South Florida.* Gainesville: University of Florida Press, 1984.

Nelson, Lowry. *Cuba: The Measure of a Revolution.* Minneapolis: University of Minnesota Press, 1972.

Perez, Louis A. *Cuba: Between Reform and Revolution.* New York: Oxford University Press, 1988.

Research Institute for Cuba. *The Cuban Immigration, 1959–1966, and Its Impact on Miami–Dade County, Florida.* Washington, D.C.: Department of Health, Education and Welfare.

Ressler, Everett M., Neil Boothby, and Daniel J. Steinbock. *Unaccompanied Children: Care and Protection in Wars, Natural Disasters, and Refugee Movements.* New York: Oxford University Press, 1988.

Suchlicki, Jaime. *Cuba: From Columbus to Castro.* New York: Scribner, 1974.

———. *University Students and Revolution in Cuba, 1920–1968.* Coral Gables: University of Miami Press, 1969.

Thomas, Hugh. *The Cuban Revolution.* New York: Harper and Row, 1977.

———. *The Spanish Civil War.* New York: Harper and Row, 1961.

Articles

Close, Kathryn. "Cuban Children Away From Home." *Children* 10 (1963): 3–10.

"Cuba: And Now the Children?" *Time,* October 6, 1961, 41.

"Cuba: Children's Crusade." *Newsweek,* April 3, 1961, 51.

"Free Transportation to U.S. Offered to Cubans with Visa Waivers." *U.S. Department of State Bulletin* 45 (August 7, 1961): 238.

Hubbell, John G. "Operacion Pedro Pan: los ninos que no esclavizo Castro" (Operation Pedro Pan: The children Castro did not enslave). *Selecciones,* May 1988, 30–34.

Hyuck, Earl, and Rona Fields. "Impact of Resettlement on Refugee Children." *International Migration Review* 15 (Spring–Summer 1981): 247–54.

Julien, Claude. "Church and State in Cuba: Development of a Conflict." *Cross Currents* (Spring 1961): 186–92.

Mitchell, William L. "The Cuban Refugee Program." *Social Security Bulletin* 25 (March 1962): 3–8.

"More about Cuban Refugee Children." *Christian Century* April 18, 1962, 479–80.

Oettinger, Katherine Brownell. "Services to Unaccompanied Cuban Refugee Children in the United States." *Social Science Review* 36 (December 1962): 377–84.

"On the Way: A Wave of Cuban Children." *U.S. News and World Report,* March 19, 1962, 16.

"President Signs Immigration Bill; Offers Asylum to Cubans." *U.S. Department of State Bulletin* 53 (October 1965): 661–63.

Reed, Gail. "Operation Pedro Pan: Flight of Fear." *Cuba Update* 15 (January–February 1994): 7–8.

"Refugee Cuban Children Need Homes." *Christian Century,* April 4, 1962, 417.

Thomas, John F. "Cuban Refugees in the United States." *International Migration Review* 1 (Fall 1966): 47–57.

———. "Cuban Refugee Program." *Welfare in Review* 1 (September 1963): 1–20.

———. "U.S.A. as Country of First Asylum." *International Migration Review* 3 (1965): 5–14.

Walsh, Bryan O. "Cubans in Miami." *America* 114 (February 26, 1966): 286–89.

———. "Cuban Refugee Children." *Journal of Inter-American Studies and World Affairs* 13 (January 1971): 379–415.

Theses and Dissertations

Adessa, Domenick Joseph. "Refugee Cuban Children: The Role of the Catholic Welfare Bureau of the Diocese of Miami, Florida, in Receiving, Caring for, and Placing Unaccompanied Cuban Children, 1960–1963." Ph.D. diss., Fordham University, 1964.

Clark, Juan. "The Exodus from Revolutionary Cuba (1959–1974): A Sociological Analysis." Ph.D. diss., University of Florida, 1975.

Masud-Piloto, Felix Roberto. "The Political Dynamics of the Cuban Migration to the United States, 1959–1980." Ph.D. diss., Florida State University, 1985.

Reports

Catholic Welfare Bureau. "Statistical Report, Year 1963." Miami, 1963.

Clark, Juan. "Cuba: Exodus, Living Conditions, and Human Rights." Brochure, Cuban American National Foundation.

First Research Corporation. "Cost Analysis of Five Institutions under Jurisdiction of the Catholic Welfare Bureau, Miami, Florida, Serving Unaccompanied Cuban Refugee Children. Based on Data Extending from January 1, 1963, to June 30, 1963." Miami, 1963.

Operation Pedro Pan Group, Inc. Brochure, printed for Thanksgiving dance, November 27, 1993.

Oettinger, Katherine B., and John F. Thomas. *Cuba's Children in Exile: The Story of the Unaccompanied Cuban Refugee Children's Program.* Washington, D.C.: Department of Health, Education and Welfare, 1967.

Speeches

Rodriguez, Lourdes. Speech given at conference "Operation Pedro Pan: History and Sociology," held by Operation Pedro Pan Group, Inc., Miami, March 21, 1992.

Walsh, Bryan O. Speech given at conference "Operation Pedro Pan: History and Sociology," held by Operation Pedro Pan Group, Inc., Miami, March 21, 1992.

Index

Alamilla, Carlos, 72
Aquino, Sixto and Vivian, 20
Areito, Grupo, 104
Arteaga, Cardinal, 33
Assumption Academy, 19
Auerbach, Frank, 20–21, 24–25

Baena, Gina, 92
Baker, James, 2, 6, 15–23, 27–28, 37, 63
Baptist Church, Cuba, 40
Bay of Pigs invasion, 28–29
Belen School, 63–64
Biscayne Boulevard Center, 64, 65
Borrego, Lourdes, 87

Cabrini Home, 86
Candelaria, Aurora, 74, 77, 87
Carrera, Maria Teresa, 71–72, 90
Carroll, Bishop Coleman F., 21
Castro, Fidel, 9, 31
Castro, Juanita, 41
Catholic Charities, National Conference of. See Catholic Welfare Bureau
Catholic Church, Cuba, 3, 6, 33

Catholic Relief Services, 66
Catholic Welfare Bureau, Diocese of Miami: awaiting children at Miami International Airport, 75–77; early role of, in Operation Pedro Pan, 18; function of, before Operation Pedro Pan, 13; help from Catholic Charities to, 65–66; services of, 56, 57; transportation of children by, 67; use of, by adult Cubans, 57–58; work of, with outside agencies, 65–67. See also Cuban Children's Program; Florida City facility; Kendall facility; Matecumbe, Camp; transit centers
children and families, Communist Cuba, 9–10
children of Operation Pedro Pan: academics, 94–95; active opposition to Castro, 4; cameraderie among, 95–96; coping mechanisms of, 93–99; emotional dependence of, on Cuban adults, 92, 93; emotions of, toward parents, 96; loneliness of, 91–93; nationalism of, 81, 96; parents of, 2–11, 70–71, 103–4; parole status

children—*continued*
of, 26; psychological impact on, 68,
87–88, 95–99; religious life of, 57,
95; reluctance of, to relocate outside Miami, 80; siblings of, 75, 95;
social class of, 2, 69–70, 90; as students, 53–54
—stages of experience: learning of departure, 70–72; *La Pecera* and departure, 72–75; arrival in Miami,
75–78; arrival at camps, 78–79;
camp life, 80–83; life at permanent
Miami homes, 83–85; orphanages,
85–86; adaptation of those sent
away, 88–91; comportment of, 90–
91; local opposition to, 91
Children's Bureau, 46, 48–51
Children's Service Bureau, 15, 55–56
Child Welfare League of America, 56
Christian Brothers, 60
Cisterna, Father Salvador de, O.F.M.,
Cap., 61
Clein, Evelyn and Ben, 55
Cleveland Plain Dealer, 66
Committees for the Defense of the
Revolution, xiii, 10
Conga del Campamento, 106
Connolly, Father William, 25–26
Cooper, Louise, 19
Crotty Brothers, 62
Cuartas, Alberto, 92, 101–2
Cuban Adjustment Act. *See* Walsh: Cu-
ban Adjustment Act
Cuban Children's Program: origins of,
2; early efforts of, 19; early funding
for, 20; and Kennedy directive, 45;
purchase of care contracts, 49–50;
definition of child refugee for pro-
gram eligibility, 50; reception of
children in Miami, 49, 75–79; funding for, 50–51; precedents for, 51–
52; use of religious schools by, 51–
52. *See also* Catholic Welfare
Bureau; Florida City facility;

Kendall facility; Matecumbe, Camp;
transit centers
Cuban Refugee Emergency Center,
15, 47.
Cuban Refugee Executive Committee,
14–15
Cuban Refugee Program, 44–48

de la Portilla, Esther, 38
de la Torriente, Elena, 42–43
del Toro, Sara 41–42
Didion, Joan, 104

education, in Cuba, 6–8
Eighth Street Center, 64
Erwin, Rachel, 26
exiles, Cuban: composition of, before
and after mid-1960, 1–2, 12; motives of, for leaving Cuba, 3–5; parole status of, 26; reasons for U.S.
stimulation of emigration, 29–30;
definition of Cuban refugee for program eligibility, 48

Feo, Hilda, 40
Ferre, Maurice, 42, 63
Finlay, Berta de la Portilla de, 36–38
Finlay, Francisco, 36–38
Florida City facility, 61–62, 80–81
Florida State Crippled Children's
Commission, 56
Florida State Department of Public
Welfare, 46, 56
Freedom Flights, 62, 100–101
Freedom Tower. *See* Cuban Refugee
Emergency Center

Garcia, Alfonso, 83–84
Giquel, Serafina, 38
Giquel, Sergio, 38
Grau, Leopoldina, 39–41
Grau Alsina, Ramon, 41
Grau San Martin, Ramon, 39
Great Britain, 23, 25, 34, 38–39

Guarch, George, 75–77

Hale, Robert F., 24
Hernandez, Moises, 84

Jamaica, 23–27
Jesuit Boys Home, 62–64, 84–85
Jewish community, U.S., and role in
Cuban Refugee Program, 15, 54–55
Jones, Robert W., 29–30
Juventud Estudiantil Catolica, 4
Juventud Obrera Catolica, 4

Kendall facility, 58–59, 81–82
Kennedy, John F., 44–46
Key West incident, 13, 14
KLM, Royal Dutch Airlines, 23, 26–
27, 35–37
Kraft, Frank, 51, 52

Ling, Martin, 77, 82
literacy campaign, 7, 8
Lost Apple, The, 78–79, 81, 92, 95, 97

Marist Brothers, 59, 67
Mas Canosa, Jorge, 47
Matecumbe, Camp, 59–61, 82–83
Menendez, Pedro, 13, 17
Merida, Daniel, 72–73, 78, 90, 95
Miro Cardona, Jose, 42
Movimiento de Rescate
Revolucionario. *See* Rescate
Revolucionario, Movimiento de
Movimiento Revolucionario del
Pueblo, 42

Netherlands, 23, 35–37

O'Farrill, Albertina, 43
Odio, Amador, 42
Opa Locka Center, 59, 64
Operation Pedro Pan: attempt to use
student visas, 17–19; end of first

phase, 22; funding for, 16, 18, 35–
36; motives for, 27–31; origins of, 2,
15–17; overall objectives of, 32–33;
and security checks, 25, 33; use of
visa waivers, 24–25, 33. *See also*
Children of Operation Pedro Pan
Operation Pedro Pan Group, Inc.,
105–6
Oteiza, Margarita, 42, 78, 82–83, 97

Padilla, Israel, 40–41
Pala, Father Francisco, 60
Panama, 34
Pecera, La. See Children of Operation
Pedro Pan: stages of experience
Perez Lopez, Beatriz, 40
Ponte, Teresa, 7, 74
Powers, Penny, 38–39, 43
Protestants, Cuba, 3

Ramudo, Luis, 81, 83
Rescate Revolucionario, Movimiento
de, 40
resettlement, Cuban refugee, 15, 47
reunification, 100–102
Ribicoff, Abraham, 44–45, 48–49, 52
Ripoll, Luis, S.J., 64, 84, 85
Rodriguez, Lourdes, 75, 94–95, 98–99
Ruston Academy, 15–16, 36–38

St. Joseph's Villa, 19
St. Raphael's, 62–63, 83–84
St. Vincent's, Brooklyn, 85
St. Vincent's, Philadelphia, 86
Sanchez, Ralph, 84
siblings, 75, 95
Swanstrom, Bishop Edward, 66
Switzerland, 34

Thomas, Alicia, 40
transit centers, 56–58, 62, 80–83. *See
also* Florida City facility; Kendall
facility; Matecumbe, Camp

underground, Cuban anti-Castro, 4,
    15–16, 33–34, 43
United Hebrew Immigrant Aid Society
    (United HIAS), 15, 54
University of Miami, 46
U.S. Highway 1 Center, 62, 64–65

Varona, Antonio, 39–40
Vilano-Chovel, Elisa, 75, 80–81, 89
visa waivers. See Operation Pedro Pan
Voorhees, Tracy, 14–15

Walsh, Bryan: and origins of Opera-
    tion Pedro Pan, 2, 13, 17–18; per-
    sonal background of, 12–13; pro-
    posal to Welfare Planning Council,
    14–15; initial meeting with James
    Baker, 16–17; and Bishop Carroll,
    21; dealings with Frank Auerbach,
21, 24–25; Cuban Adjustment Act,
    26; and Jamaica trip, 26–27; smug-
    gling visas into Cuba, 33; helping
    families purchase airline tickets,
    35–36; meeting with Sara del Toro,
    42; meeting with Ribicoff, 48–49;
    development of transit centers, 58–
    62; San Raphael's, 62–63, 83–84.
    See also Cuban Children's Program;
    Operation Pedro Pan
Welfare Planning Council, 14, 15
Wolins, Martin, 51

Yaballi, Sara, 92–98
youth organizations, Communist
    Cuba, 5–6

Zayas, Elvira Jované de, 40